Dream Home

Kimberley W. Bush

DEDICATION

This book is dedicated to my children; Jaida, Jarod and Julian.
I hope we were able to teach you some valuable lessons about
faith.

CONTENTS

ACKNOWLEDGMENTS

First and foremost, thank you God for always sending me what I needed when I needed it whether I understood at the time or not.

I want to thank my husband and mighty man of valor, Steven Bush, for putting up with me and my computer on all those nights. I want to thank my mother, Patricia D. Williams, for always being there no matter what.

Thank you to Pastors Wayne and Linda Powe of R.A.M. Ministries for adopting me, teaching me how to enjoy my marriage, helping me heal, covering me and my family in prayer and being my trusted source of wise and godly counsel.

Thank you to my pastor, Dr. Hart Ramsey, for pastoring us in the true spirit of a shepherd. The powerful revelations of God's word through your messages at Northview Christian Church – Safe Harbor and your tireless dedication to the HRM Mentorship Class are invaluable. Thank you to Alethia Ramsey for being a willing vessel and speaking things into my life that ultimately led to the resurrection of this project after I thought it would never be published. Thank you to Precious R. Freeman for designing my cover art.

Thank you to Pastor Leonard Slater, First Lady Dianne Slater and all the saints of Family Life Bible Fellowship Church. The priceless contributions you made to our lives are too numerous to count.

Thank you to all of my past clients for allowing me the privilege to serve as your Realtor. It was an honor to be entrusted with one of the biggest investments you'll ever make. Finally, I want to thank all my clients, friends and family that supported me, referred others to me and encouraged me. I couldn't have done it without your love, prayers and help!

Kimberley W. Bush

PREFACE

It seems that I've been writing for as long as I can remember. From the first journals I kept up until now, it has always been easier to write my feelings than speak them. Like most people, I've had some tragedy in my life, some deep hurts but twice as many blessings. We can't have sunshine without some rain, right? Such is the nature of life! By the time we got to the point of wanting to build a house, so many other things had happened that we knew God would do it for us. When the house was almost done, God instructed me to document everything that had happened in the process. I just continued as it went along and wrote a little after each stage was completed.

There were days after the story was done (or so I thought) that I would pull it out and read it again to remind me of what God had done for us. Building the house was the first of many tests that would come. We thought that once the house was built and we were moved in everything would be peachy. Little did we know that God was about to start building our faith even more. Just as any loving father would, he took us by the hand and taught us how to walk.

My prayer for this book is that it will stir up the faith of every person that reads it. I hope the description of what I felt led to do and the end result is practical enough that you can apply it to any area of your life. I hope that you rediscover your dreams and get the nerve to ask God to guide you in pursuing them. Be blessed!

1 BACK TO SCHOOL

Deciding to go to real estate school was a difficult decision. I tell people that I felt God leading me to do it until I finally stepped out. He didn't tell me in a 'burning bush' kind of way; it was more of a gentle nudging. One night after church, one of the ladies I greatly respected came up to me and asked, "Are you thinking about going back to school?" I laughed and said, "Yes, but I can't decide if I should go back to college or real estate school." She pointed at me while looking me straight in the eye, "Go to real estate school. Talk to your husband first. But your kids are about to get out of school for the summer, this is the perfect time." Then she turned and gathered her things to leave without saying another word.

I started looking through the phone book the next day. At the time, my daughter Jaida was eight, my sons Jarod and Julian were five and barely three years old. I was working full time at a small business. We were active in our church and life never seemed to slow down long enough for me to take a deep breath. I wondered when I would have time to study for my license between work, taking care of my family and all of my other responsibilities. Ultimately, I understood that God would give me the strength to do it if He placed the desire in me.

I stopped by a local real estate school after I picked up my daughter from school one afternoon. Their schedule seemed like the easiest one I could manage. I would only have to attend the pre-license classes one night per week for a three hour session. The best part was that I could start during any week I chose. When I had taken all the required sessions then I could take the instructor's practice test. Once I passed the practice test then I could register for the state test. My husband and I discussed it and he agreed to support me. I enrolled in April of 2006 and faced my fears head on for the first time in years.

At first, juggling school and life was a challenge. Class days felt like they might never end until my kids were finally out of school for the summer. I would leave home at 7:00 in the morning to drop off my children at two different schools. Then I drove back across town through horrendous traffic trying to get to work by 8:30 on a good day. At 2:30 pm I would head out to pick up my daughter first and then pick up the boys. We went home and my mom, who was living with us at the time, would usually have dinner ready if she could. If not, I made dinner for us. We did homework if the kids had any, I ran their baths and my husband took over. By 5:30 I was driving back across town to class. Class started at 6:00 pm and we got one or two breaks before it ended at 9:00 but I loved it.

The distance from our home to Jaida's school was about thirty miles one way. When she was in school that meant I could drive a total of 180 miles in one day. I put some serious miles on my poor minivan! When summer came, I only had to make that trip once a week. When August rolled around I was well into a routine and I felt less overwhelmed. I completed all my courses by September and I took a whole month to study before I tackled the practice test. It only took two attempts for me to pass and I got the certificate of completion I needed to register for the state license exam.

The morning of my state exam, I did the same thing I had done on the morning of the practice test. I took the whole day off, went to a diner and had a good breakfast first. I looked over some of the chapters of my textbook and said a prayer. I was nervous and scared. I wasn't really sure what I would do after I got my license. In my mind, I just had to finish. In 32 years I had never really finished anything I started. I went into the testing area and there were three of us taking the exam that day. We introduced ourselves and I recognized the name of the lady to my left. I had spoken to many Realtors through my work at my full time job. This lady was already a Realtor in a town south of us and she was there to take her broker exam.

Pretty soon, the proctor came in and explained the time we would be given to complete the test. He made a few jokes to ease our minds and whether we were ready or not he started the program on the computers in front of us. I tried not to over think my answers and listen to the little voice that was telling me which answers to choose. Before I knew it, I had answered all 145 questions. I still had thirty minutes left so I went back and checked all my answers. I was terrified that I had failed but I hit the 'finished' button and got up from the computer.

When I went out into the hallway, the jolly proctor came out of his office and we walked into the room where my results were printing. He said excitedly, "I know you passed!" I shrugged and tried to resist the urge to throw up. It seemed like the paper would never stop coming out of the laser printer. When it finally did, the proctor took it out and read over the first few pages. I needed a 70 or better to pass and I was holding my breath while he looked for my score. He grinned and handed me the temporary license page. I exhaled when I saw my score of 76. I was stunned and relieved at the same time.

I walked out of the testing center and turned my phone back on so I could call Steve. He congratulated me and said, "I knew you could do it!" I told him I had doubted it the whole time I was taking the test especially since I finished so early. We talked for a few minutes and I decided to treat myself to a manicure and pedicure. Ironically, the test wasn't the hard part. The hardest thing I would have to do was yet to come. I knew I couldn't do real estate part time for long. There was already some tension at work because I couldn't put in full time hours. Once it came out about me becoming a Realtor it would only be a matter of time before I had to make another tough decision.

Only a small group of family and friends knew I was going to school. I felt I had to keep it a secret because I knew some wouldn't agree with my decision. I had worked the same job for ten years and everyone just assumed I would do that for the rest of my life. The only problem with that was it was someone else's dream and not mine. When I turned thirty I had an epiphany. I realized that I had lost myself somewhere between the diapers, sleepless nights, doctor appointments and various therapy visits. I had married young and started a family early so I never had the single, independent years to find out who I was and what my purpose was. I felt that God wanted me to rekindle the desires of my heart with His help. After all, He didn't give us imaginations for nothing. God intended for us to dream!

Just like Joseph in the book of Genesis I had told people my dreams in the past and had them shot down when they didn't agree. In chapter 37, Joseph described his dream to his brothers and they didn't agree with it. They hated Joseph when they realized their father loved him more than his other children. Not learning his lesson the first time, Joseph told them about his dream again. By this time their hatred had grown to the point they wanted Joseph dead. The same thing can happen to us when we share our dreams with people and give them authority to speak into our lives. It may not be a literal death but they will plant seeds of doubt in our minds that will cause us to abandon our dreams for mediocrity.

I had already decided to put my license with a small company that a friend worked for part time. When I got my temporary license, I ordered business cards and it was official! I was so proud of my cards but I still had one more step to take. I had to take post-license classes to get my permanent license. So, I enrolled in the same school for the 30 hour class. By now, I figured it was time to come clean at work. I mustered up my courage and walked into the owner's office one day. I put my business card in the middle of his desk and said, "I have my real estate license now and I'll be working for this company. I just thought you should know." After that, things were even more complicated but I couldn't un-ring the bell.

I took steps to get started and I was having more fun than I ever thought possible in the process. I joined the local Realtor's Association and ordered a used Palm Pilot for my electronic lockbox key. I learned how to use MLS and research properties. In my spare time I started working on my next mission, finding us a new house! Over the next year, many things transpired before I finally resigned from my full time job in December of 2007. Change is not always easy, especially when the future you expected is totally different from the one you find yourself living out. I took a full twenty one days to pray and fast for wisdom before I actually turned in my letter of resignation but we'll get into that later. As a result, I came out stronger, wiser and more determined than ever to succeed in my new career.

Months before I ever enrolled in real estate school, I was getting ready for work one morning. It was just like any other morning when suddenly I heard this still, small voice say, "Start getting plans ready for your house." At the time, we had been living in Steve's childhood home for about three years. I thought about this for a minute and decided that I would like to remodel the house and make it more functional. God had to be more specific because He knows I'm slow in the mornings. "Get your plans ready for your new house. When you move in, everything will be brand new." At that point, I had to sit down.

At that time, we had been attending our church for about a year and as a result we had become faithful tithers. Inspired and motivated by the teaching we received I began to dream again. As I said before, my imagination had been on life support from years of financial hardship and dealing with three sick children. One Sunday, a young woman shared her testimony of getting her first house. She said she sat down with her husband and made a list of everything they wanted in their new home. When they started house hunting they were shocked to find a house that had every one of the 22 things on their list.

I went home and typed out a list of things based on conversations I had with my husband. I read it to him later that night and we agreed that we had put all of our requirements on the list. Pretty soon, I began to cut pictures out of magazines or print them from the Internet and put them into a binder. As the weeks went by, my binder got too full to close. I moved up to a bigger binder. I started ordering faucet and furniture catalogs online. For the cover, I printed out one of my favorite scriptures and glued the color rendering of my favorite house plan below it. Psalm 37:4 says, "Delight yourself in the Lord and He will give you the desires of your heart."

That may sound crazy but what sounds more insane is the fact that we had filed chapter 7 bankruptcy three months earlier. Years of medical bills, expensive prescriptions and special schooling for our daughter had taken a toll on our finances. We also had not been tithing during that time. We lost the house we had been renting out since our move to Steve's childhood home. Then we had to default on several credit cards and loans. Through God's grace and mercy we were already living in another house and had no worries of having our possessions put out on the curb. Usually, people that file chapter 7 and owe creditors as much as we did find themselves without a home and the basic necessities. However, God showed us favor from the moment we rededicated our lives to Him.

Our pastor taught us about faith in the face of any situation. We believed that our house was out there and when the timing was right, we would get it. Some of the members at church shared their testimonies of losing houses and filing bankruptcy. It gave me hope that if God brought them through that, He would do it for us too. They had been restored and even bought houses again. I'm sure we all know that visions and dreams need time to manifest. As long as the earth remains, there will be seed, time and harvest. In order to push me on further, God gave me another nudge while I was getting ready for work on yet another morning. A pastor on television was teaching on Abraham and I was half-listening until I heard, "Get thee from thy father's house and from thy country to a land that I will show thee..." That particular verse really got my attention. The only way I can describe it is I felt it in my gut. From that point I started thinking outside the box.

With my newly minted real estate license and electronic lockbox key I started looking at houses every chance I got. I didn't have any clients yet but I took some time to get familiar with all the neighborhoods in our city. Sometimes I took my daughter with me to preview properties and we had so much fun. I would go to furniture stores and daydream, picking out what I wanted as if I already had enough money to get it. Years later I realized how great the power of my faith in God was in those days. I searched the MLS endlessly and looked at hundreds of pictures and virtual tours in our existing home inventory. I was discovering a love for research that I never knew I possessed.

In late February of 2007 I got a phone call one evening while I was making dinner for my kids. The man on the other end said he wanted me to help him purchase a home. He said his name was James and he said he got my number from a local magazine that I had advertised in. When he described the logo in the ad I knew he had an old copy. By this time I had moved my license to another company that specialized in new construction and custom built homes. I asked him some questions and we chatted for a few minutes. He said he had gone to his pastor for advice on buying a home. His pastor was the one that gave him the magazine and told him to call me. The strange thing was, I had never even met or heard of his pastor! I took down his information and promised to call him back the next day so we could get him pre-qualified for a mortgage. I could barely contain my excitement over my very first client!

One of my friends, Mr. Baker, had just started in the mortgage business. He needed new clients as badly as I did so I referred James to him. I hoped Mr. Baker would be able to give us some good news. Thankfully, he was able to help James resolve his credit issues and get him approved for a loan. I was so excited! I was hopeful we could find something really nice for him and his wife. James was anxious to get started and I got a crash course in learning how to sell homes. I hadn't had much training yet and I basically relied on my instincts. On top of that my broker had been selling new homes for years and existing homes was a little different. We never got a chance to talk about training and I didn't know what questions to ask anyway.

James and I muddled through even though his lack of computer savvy and an email address made my job even more challenging. One evening James called me wanting information on several homes. He had picked up one of those free home magazines from a store. As a sidebar, most agents consider those books to be a blessing or a curse; it just depends on the day you ask. Anyway, James gave me descriptions of the houses he liked and asked me to give him the prices. It didn't take long for both of us to get frustrated. I'll admit that I do not advise any agent to do what I did next.

James was not familiar with the part of town where my office was and it was getting dark. He wanted answers and I felt obligated to give them to him. I didn't want to lose my first client, especially when he was qualified to actually buy something. I invited James to my home so we could look at his book together. I felt he was harmless and my husband was at home with me. What happened after he got there was like something out of The Three Stooges. My computer was in my bedroom so I left James at my dining room table while I ran back and forth to search the MLS for the homes he had circled on various pages in the book. Most of the homes didn't have an address or even a hint of the location. Finally, I explained to him that I would search all the homes in his price range and we would go look at some of them on Saturday. Before he left, I invited him back for dinner on Sunday when some of our church family would be there. James did come and I think he really enjoyed himself. He even discovered one of the members was a former co-worker and they had a ball.

When the day came to look at the houses I was nervous to the point of being almost overwhelmed. I had only previewed homes alone up until this point so having to actually "show" a house was new to me. That's another thing we don't learn in school. James brought his wife and his stepson and we met at a shopping center near the neighborhood we would be looking in. They opted to follow me in their car and off we went. I had chosen about four houses for us to see and ironically the first one was only three blocks from the church we were attending at the time. As soon as we walked through the back door into the kitchen, James declared the search was over. He hadn't even seen the other houses and he was asking about making an offer. I jokingly said, "But this is the first one we've seen!" James didn't care, he and his wife acted like this house was a mansion compared to where they were presently living.

I went to my car and got the contract so we could write it up immediately. I went back to my office to fax it to the listing agent and we waited eagerly for a response. We haggled over the price and terms for a couple of days before everyone agreed. The closing date was set for April 16, 2007. James had a home inspection done and the sellers agreed to make some minor repairs. When closing day came I was ecstatic. James and his family were getting a home they loved and I was getting a check! The closing went off without a hitch and I almost shouted for joy when the last document was signed.

2 SUPERNATURAL SUCCESS

Even though I was selling real estate part time, the market was okay and God blessed me that first year. I was working in the smallest neighborhood my company marketed and doing open houses on Sundays after church. That spring my company participated in the Parade of Homes and that meant open houses every day for two weeks. One Saturday afternoon I was in one of the houses and the traffic was incredible. I had put dozens of balloons and directional signs out and it obviously worked. Later that day right before it was time to close up I met a lovely lady with long, silver hair named Liz. She was quietly walking through the home I was hosting and looking at everything. I sidled up to her and made small talk. She was a widow and she wanted to move into a new house and start over. She loved the location, the floor plan and all the other features of the house. I couldn't get her to commit but I gave her my card and asked her to sign our guest register.

A week or so passed and the Parade of Homes ended. One Sunday I was having dinner with some friends from our church. Just as we prepared to bless the meal my phone rang. It was the agent in charge of the neighborhood I had been subbing in. The answering service had called her because someone wanted to see a house. She was working in a different neighborhood across town that day and she wanted to know if I could handle the call. I explained my situation and how it would be at least an hour before I was free so she reluctantly decided to call the customer and meet them herself. I wondered if I was missing out on a sale but God had me covered. The customer turned out to be Liz and she told the listing agent all about me and how much she had enjoyed chatting with me.

To make a long story short, Liz bought that house she loved so much and since I had met her first the listing agent suggested to our broker that I get the selling side of the commission! I had the honor of meeting with Liz to get the contract signed. I did the footwork since the listing agent was busy with a different subdivision that was selling faster. I was grateful for the chance to learn how new construction worked. I attended the closing and handled the paperwork so we both could get paid. It was a valuable experience that I will always remember.

We had another house down the street from the one Liz moved into. It was owned by the same builder and they really needed to sell. One morning I drove into the neighborhood and looked at that house. God reminded me of the story of Israel marching around Jericho seven times. I got out of my car and took off. There was a construction crew working across the street but I didn't care who saw me. I walked around that house seven times, praying all the way. When I was finished I got back in my car and left. The next week I was in the office late one evening and I heard a contract had come in on that house. I let out a shout of victory and the other agents looked at me like I was nuts. The listing agent handled it all and I didn't get paid but it was one less house for me to open and close on the weekends.

My next client was a lady in our church. She wanted a new home and she was already working with an online mortgage company. This was my first introduction to the truth of the phrase, "real estate is local". The loan officer she had been dealing with was completely ignorant about some aspects of our local market. She had grossly over estimated property taxes for our area. Alabama has some of the lowest property taxes in the country. When I pointed out the error, she was gracious but it set off alarm bells for me. When we got our good faith estimate of the total charges associated with the loan, the private mortgage insurance was twice as high as the property tax estimate. It was going to kill the sale because my client wouldn't be able to afford the monthly payments.

I called a mortgage company that had been helpful to me personally in the past and got a better good faith estimate with more realistic tax and PMI amounts. My buyer was relieved and I knew we would make it to the closing table. Once she took all of her documents to the new loan officer we got a pre-approval letter and headed out to find her home. We went to a neighborhood she had been admiring for a while and looked at three or four homes. After she took a few days to pray about it she decided on one, we wrote up the offer and got it accepted by the end of the week.

The builder agreed to purchase an appliance for her and have it installed by closing. When we did our walk-through he went over all the features of her new home and gave her his contact info. He was providing a one year warranty and he urged her to call him if she had any problems. Within a month I was at the closing table again, watching someone's dream come true. I can't describe what it feels like but I never get tired of it. Now that things were picking up for me, I was really enjoying the extra income. We were even able to take a short trip as a family. It had been at least two years since we were able to do that; before our third child was born.

Every once in a while I have a dream that stays with me for days afterwards. One night I dreamt I was in a two-story house and the second floor had a bonus room. The kitchen was everything I wanted and the whole house was beautifully decorated. I walked through the entire house but I wasn't sure if I lived there. I went downstairs and out the front door. The house appeared to be on a corner lot. Suddenly I heard children and when I turned to look there were several children passing by on bikes. When I woke up I wrote the details of the dream in my journal and forgot all about it.

My next client was a close friend and she wanted to look for a house she could retire in. Once again I was slightly challenged because she didn't have an email address or knowledge of the Internet. With all the technology we have these days most of the elimination process can be done through email without ever leaving home. However she needed to see and touch the product in order to get a good feel for it. So off we trekked through all of the semi-rural areas in our county plus the two flanking us. We were standing outside a house talking after the showing one day when a small group of children rode by on bicycles just like in my dream. The eerie thing was I recognized the kids! They were the children of some friends of ours and they lived right down the street. That event solidified my belief that this was the area we would live in.

One Saturday my friend and I spent three hours going from one side of the River Region to the other looking at homes. By the time we saw the last one I was already late for my open house. We drove past a house that looked vacant but I didn't have time to stop. I promised her I would look it up later and call her with the details. When I went online to research the house I discovered it had been listed with three different companies over the last two years. There weren't many interior photos but I could tell it was close to what my friend wanted. I called her at 10:30 that night, something that was out of character for me but I was sure in my gut it was the one. We set a time to go back and see it after church the next day.

In the early years my family went with me on some weekend appointments out of necessity, being that we only had one vehicle the five of us could fit into. We made the twenty minute drive to the suburb the house was located in and everybody was eager to see inside. As soon as I opened the door, we all kept shaking our heads in amazement. The formal living areas and the kitchen had 25 foot ceilings at least. There was a gathering room off the kitchen with a fireplace. All the floors were tile except the bedrooms which had carpet, exactly what she wanted. The master bedroom was about seventeen feet by twenty-five feet. The master bath was absolutely gorgeous. We were giggling and talking when my friend nudged me and nodded in my husband's direction. He wasn't saying much but I could tell he was impressed. He saw firsthand that it was possible for us to live in a home like this one.

Up until this point, the wish book I had created for our dream home was kind of my thing just between me and God. Steve had listened politely while I rambled on about oil-rubbed bronze plumbing fixtures. However I don't think he could see us in a home like the one we were standing in. But I could tell his faith was growing from watching someone else exercise their faith. Needless to say this house was definitely the one and we left knowing we would make an offer on it as soon as possible. The seller was a tough negotiator and the reason he was selling made it more complicated. Eventually, he relented and accepted our offer. We closed in late July and I walked away knowing I had found the community we wanted to raise our family in.

After that closing, I spent a lot of time looking at the inventory in the area where my friend purchased her home. Because of the bankruptcy we still couldn't apply for a mortgage so we worked on rebuilding our credit. Out of curiosity I looked at the active listings in the neighborhood where I saw our friends' children. There was a house available that looked very similar to the one I saw in my dream. I was still working full time so I took my lunch break to go see it and I took Steve back the next day. When I walked in the door I was blown away by hand shaved wood floors, the light fixtures and the overall grandeur. It was better than my dream even though there was no furniture. However, God will sometimes allow us to see things that we've asked for just to stir up our faith. As Ephesians 3:20 says, He wants us to know that He can do more than anything we ask or think. Although the house was my dream home, the price was out of our range. Proverbs 10:22 says,

"The blessing of the Lord makes one rich and adds no sorrow with it." It felt like our house but the timing wasn't right.

I went to get my hair done one night and my stylist introduced me to one of her clients. The lady said she had a co-worker that wanted to sell their starter house and move up. She told me a little about what they were looking for and I gave her my card. The co-worker, whose name was Jamie, called me the next day and I had new clients again! Jamie and I hit it off immediately. I was excited about my first listing. Jamie and her husband Dan wanted a new home for their growing family.

I went over on a Saturday to look at their house and give them some suggestions. They had made the best use of the space and it was immaculate. Jamie had decorated their son's room and I could tell they took pride in maintaining their house. It was freshly painted and the small yard was manicured to perfection. I could see we would have some challenges because they lived in a town home and it only had two bedrooms. But I knew with the condition and the location we could get it sold with the right marketing. I put it on the market the next week. We didn't get many showings but I warned them it might take time because the house was only two bedrooms. In the meantime I emailed Jamie some houses that I thought they might like.

They were honest with me about their situation and I sent them to Mr. Baker because I knew he could help them. Mr. Baker got them approved for a mortgage and we looked at some houses. Dan and Jamie wanted to bring both sets of parents back to see their final three choices. One house was in one of the neighborhoods my company marketed but it backed up to a major road. Jamie was concerned that they wouldn't be able to enjoy their backyard but Dan didn't seem to care. The parents just wanted the kids to be happy. The next one was in a different new home neighborhood but it was built during the first phase of construction. The house had been updated but Dan and Jamie liked the neighborhood more than the house. The last one was in the same neighborhood but in the current phase and it was brand new. It had four bedrooms plus a bonus room off the kitchen that Jamie planned to use as an office. In the end, Dan and Jamie chose the brand new house.

A few months went by and we had two showings. Dan and Jamie were getting a little weary of the waiting game. Since I was a rookie and hadn't had much training I did something really dumb. Jamie was worried that when their house finally sold the house they wanted would be sold too. She asked if they could just go ahead and make an offer on their dream house. I didn't know what else to do so I agreed and we wrote up the offer. I sent it to the listing agent and she called me as soon as she got it. She was a typical "type A" personality and she wasn't trying to hide her irritation. "I got your offer and I have some questions," she said. I said, "Okay." "Have they gotten an offer on their home yet?" I couldn't lie so I said, "No, but we're confident we can get it sold. They really want this house and when they do sell they can't wait six months for another one to be built." The listing agent said she couldn't negotiate their offer until their house was sold or at least had an offer on it. I reluctantly gave Jamie the news but I reassured her that she would get her house.

Another month went by and the year was slowly coming to a close. Around this time the market is always slow but it was the beginning of the end for the good old days in real estate. The listing agent for the house Dan and Jamie wanted called me one day with a proposition. She said, "Are your people still interested in the house?" I could barely contain my excitement but I kept my game face on, "Well, what is the builder offering?" She explained that the builder would buy their house but they wouldn't get fair market value. With their current mortgage satisfied they would be free to purchase the house they wanted. I said, "Let me talk to my clients and I'll call you back." She blurted out something about this proposal having a time limit so I assured her she would hear from me soon.

I called Jamie and when she answered the phone I said, "Are you sitting down?" She said, "Yes, why?" I relayed the details of my conversation with the listing agent and she said, "Oh my goodness! I've gotta talk to Dan. I'll call you back." Ten minutes later Dan called and asked me to explain everything again. I patiently gave him the play by play of my conversation with the other agent. He said, "Let us discuss it some more and we'll call you back." Jamie called me back an hour later and said they wanted to go for it. I thanked God profusely before I composed myself and called the other agent to tell her it was a go. She said she would take the builder to see it the next day and let me know. I knew that Dan and Jamie would have the house ready but I called them to give a heads up. That next afternoon I was on pins and needles waiting for the other agent to call me back. When she finally did, it was great news. "The house showed well and they've kept it up nicely. The builder is ready to proceed if they are," she said. I told her we were ready to go.

I went to Dan and Jamie's house that night and we rewrote the contract. I got it to the other agent's office and waited for her to send it back to me. They went to see Mr. Baker to get their final paperwork done. Mr. Baker worked to get them a final approval but a problem came up and their file was held up in the underwriting department. Mr. Baker was still new at the mortgage business but he had worked in sales for most of his life. He told me to try my best to keep Dan and Jamie calm but it was getting harder with each passing day. I couldn't give them or the listing agent an answer about when we could close for sure. As the days wore on everybody called me constantly but I didn't know what to tell them. One night Jamie called and said the listing agent had just called her at home. She had demanded to know if they were going to buy the house or not. I was livid and so were they.

I called the listing agent and asked her why she had called my clients. I explained that their loan officer was working as hard as he could but the investor that was financing the loan was located in California. With the time difference they were coming in to work when Mr. Baker was already tied up with phone calls and other deals. Then when Mr. Baker tried to contact them they were out to lunch. It was a huge mess and I was right in the middle of it. I told her to call me from then on and to leave my clients alone. Mr. Baker and I talked briefly at church and he told me he had never seen anything like it before. We were both praying hard for this loan to close soon. We went ahead with the walk-through on the scheduled day but we still didn't know anything. The other agent pulled me aside the first chance she got to ask if I had heard anything. I admitted that we still didn't have an answer.

Two days later we were still on standby but Dan and Jamie showed up at the closing attorney's office anyway. They called me every hour to see if I had any news. In the heat of the moment Dan and Mr. Baker said some things to each other that compounded everybody's stress. I left work to go to the attorney's office to see if I could help. I called Mr. Baker to see what was going on and when he told me what they had said to each other I began to dread facing Dan with nothing to report. When I walked in the door Dan and Jamie were holding a vigil in the reception area. I felt horrible but there was really nothing I could do. Mr. Baker called me to say he still didn't have a package for the closing so we might as well go home. I relayed his message to Dan and Jamie and I saw her lip start to quiver, tears threatening to spill onto her cheeks at any minute. Then the attorney came out and told us the same thing. Dan was fuming and he was quite abrupt when I tried to reassure them. He jumped into his car and drove off.

I got in my car and resisted the urge to cry. I went home and told Steve the whole sad story. He told me that God would work it all out. His words proved true a few days later. I got a call from Mr. Baker saying he had found the problem. Apparently the documents provided by the other agent's company had the wrong legal address. The underwriters had no idea the title work wasn't matching up because they were trying to deed the wrong property. Mr. Baker said he had kept praying the night before and asking, "What is it Lord? Why can't we get this sale closed?" He woke up the next morning and felt the need to look over all the documents from the sale again and that was when he caught the discrepancy. I couldn't believe it. Mr. Baker said the package was on its way to the attorney and even though he liked to attend closings he was going to sit this one out. After what happened between him and Dan, I felt that was best.

We got to the closing and discovered we were going to have a "dry" closing. That's the term for a closing where no checks are issued. We signed the paperwork and exchanged keys but the agents didn't get paid. I was just happy the ordeal was over for Dan and Jamie. They had gotten their dream house just like I knew they would. After the closing we walked outside and I congratulated Dan and Jamie. Dan looked like he had something to say all through the closing and now he wanted to unburden his conscience. He apologized for his behavior and I knew he was sincere. People sometimes shock themselves with their behavior when they're under pressure. I assured Dan that he didn't need to apologize but he insisted. I shook his hand and gave Jamie a hug. Jamie and I kept in contact and even though I tried to keep in touch with both of them, they listed their home with someone else when they relocated a few years later.

3 STEPPING OUT

In the spring of 2007 while I was subbing in the neighborhood again a lady came into the construction trailer that served as our site office with her agent. She wanted to see which lots were available. I showed her a plat map and gave her some plans to choose from. She had been inside our largest model home before and that was the one she wanted. I offered to take her inside again to get a feel for the plan but she said it wouldn't be necessary. So we walked the lots and I pointed out the boundaries since the high grass was covering some of the engineer's stakes. She picked a lot, signed a lot reservation form and wrote out a check for the lot binder that day.

By late October her custom built home was all finished. There had been many changes to the plan but everyone was happy. That turned out to be my last closing for the year and even though I split it with the listing agent it was still a sizable amount of money. I continued to work my full time job and sell real estate part time but it was becoming obvious that I wouldn't be able to do both for much longer. Matthew 6:24 says that no man can serve two masters because he will eventually love one and hate the other. For the first time I was beginning to understand this verse very clearly. In the scripture that verse is talking about people that love money more than they love God and end up seeing money as their god. Still, it was a fitting description for what I was going through. Some of the leaders at our church didn't want me to leave my full time job but they didn't understand that doing both was not an option. They assumed I could just take off for closings or real estate related things when I needed to do. However, my job didn't offer annual leave or paid time off because it was a small business. When the hours on the door said we were open they expected me to be there.

When I was with my clients on the weekends and driving all over the River Region in my minivan life was exciting and fulfilling. When I went to work Monday through Friday I felt like I was being punished. While the steady paycheck helped to provide for my family I was ready to trust God with the sporadic commission checks from real estate. My husband wasn't at that level of faith yet and there was tension between us because of it. After I sold my friend her house that was the most money I had made in my whole life at one time. It would have taken me nearly six months to earn that much at my full time job. But I kept going to work every day mainly to keep the peace at home. My husband was the head of our house and we both knew the proper order of marriage. I knew God wouldn't bless the work of my hands if I made a major financial move without my husband's approval.

At the time I was confiding heavily in a trusted counselor and mentor. She was advising me on how to pray and what to do while I waited for God to manifest the things I had been praying for. After much discussion I decided to go on a fast to receive revelation and guidance from God. In the book of Daniel, chapter ten, Daniel had been on a fast for three weeks or twenty-one days when the angel of the Lord came to him with a message. That message was the answer to a prayer that Daniel had prayed at the beginning of his consecration before the Lord. Many Christians follow Daniel's example when they want a specific answer to a specific prayer or situation. So while I was fasting from sweets, meat and bread I concentrated on reading my bible, praying for an answer to my situation and praying for everyone involved to be at peace.

I believe that when a person makes a decision to secretly go on a fast God will answer the prayer they put before Him and many others that they might have forgotten about. I believe Matthew 6:18 when it says God will reward you in public for what you've done in private. I got confirmation that the date of December 31, 2007 was my last day working at my full time job. Steve knew I was fasting for an answer and he didn't argue or even question me when I told him what I felt led to do. I typed my resignation and instead of the customary two week notice I gave a whole month's notice. The lady that would basically assume the bulk of my responsibilities had only been with us for about eight months. I knew she needed to ask me questions and I wanted to try and give her as many answers as I could. Overall, the transition wasn't as tumultuous as I had envisioned. To my great surprise I was given a going away party. In fact, I was so surprised that when they asked me to say a few words I really couldn't think of anything to say.

In January of 2008 I was enjoying my freedom to work in real estate and focus on learning more about the resale market. The new home market was slowly drying up and I figured I had better switch gears to adapt when the change came. One day my "check engine" light came on in the minivan. It wasn't unusual since we had to have the exact same repair done on the van every summer. Also, no matter what kind of battery we put in that van it only lasted a year at the most. I assumed it was another sensor or hose that needed to be replaced. I made an appointment with the dealer and took it in the next day. My daughter happened to be out of school that day so she went with me to get the van checked out. I have to backtrack and say that for the last two years of my full time job I had a poster of my dream car over my desk. It was a three page fold-out of a Nissan Armada in silver with the chrome package.

Some days when I was on the phone or on hold with a supplier I would lean back in my chair and gaze up at that poster. I was perfectly content to keep driving my minivan but whenever God wanted to bless me with that Armada I wasn't going to turn Him down. On the morning of the service appointment with the dealer I was pulling into a parking space when I saw it. It was 7:30 in the morning and the sun was just barely up. I glanced to my right as I was parking and through a haze of foggy smoke coming from the back of the service garage I saw the silver Nissan Armada with a chrome bumper, just like the one from my poster, parked in the back of the 'used' lot. I stopped mid-park, blinked and said, "Oh my God…" I said it in such a way that Jaida asked, "What is it Mommy?" I came back from my daze and muttered, "That's my car over there."

We went inside and signed in and since I knew the service department clerk well, he greeted me by name. Jaida and I sat down to wait and I tried to get up the courage to inquire about the price of the Armada. When the minivan was finished an hour or so later they called me to the service desk to pay. Interestingly, they couldn't find anything wrong with the van. I timidly asked the receptionist, "Do you know how much they're asking for the Nissan Armada out back?" She said, "No, but let me call a salesman for you." I almost said, "No, that's okay!" The salesman came over and asked me if I wanted to take it for a test drive. I asked him about the price but he kept talking about all the features. He crowed while rubbing his hands together, "Man, this thing is fully loaded!" I figured if I did test drive it at least I could say I drove one before I died so I relented. Thinking back on it now, it's hilarious how I had faith to leave a steady job but I didn't have faith that God could give me my dream car.

The salesman went off to find the keys and I was grinning like an idiot. Jaida asked, "Mommy, what are we doing?" "We're about to take this car for a test drive, "I said. Anyone that knows Jaida can tell you that this was not the end of the questions so I explained what that meant while we waited for the man to come back with the keys. Pretty soon, we were clicking our seatbelts and off we went. Driving that truck was so much fun. Since I'm very short, I liked being up high enough to look down into other cars as they passed by. I couldn't resist the growing laughter that threatened to spill out at any moment so I giggled like a little kid. We made it back to the dealership and the salesman went into his pitch. I told him that unless he gave me a price we didn't have much to talk about. He went to talk to his boss. As it turned out, the Armada had been traded in the day before and they hadn't decided on a price yet.

I realized how much time had gone by so I called Steve to tell him about the Armada. We laughed like it was the funniest joke we'd ever heard. By that time the salesman was coming back with his boss so I told Steve I would call him back. The manager invited me into his office and the salesman asked for my van keys so they could get a quick appraisal. He gave me a price and I said, "What kind of payments are we talking about?" He said, "That would be around $780 a month." I said, "Oh no, my husband would never go for that." But the auto industry was suffering just like the housing market was. It was the first of the year, January 7th to be exact, and they probably hadn't met last year's projected sales goals. They kept throwing out numbers until I finally said, "Okay, I won't waste any more of your time. If you just give me my keys back I'll get out of your way."

They wanted to sell me that truck as badly as I wanted to

drive it home. The manager said, "I tell you what, take the truck and let your husband see it. Let him appreciate the value before we negotiate anymore." I let out a chuckle and said, "Sir, we're talking about somebody that has held on to a 1990 Nissan 240 SX with a blown head gasket for the last three years because it was his first new car. It's been sitting in our driveway because he can't bear to part with it. I think he can appreciate value." I smiled as I added, "He is not going to pay more than $500 a month for this car. I don't care how nice it is." The manager said, "Well, we can't do that." I told him I understood and I got up to leave. "Wait", he said, "Just take it anyway. If he doesn't like it just bring it back before we close tonight." I agreed and Jaida and I drove away smiling.

My first stop was my mom's apartment about a mile away. Jaida asked me, "Mommy are they gonna let us keep this car?" I explained that if they didn't sell it to us for the right price we would be giving it back. I laughed so hard when she said, "If we can't keep it I'm gonna cry." Just then we pulled up to my mom's place. I called her on my cell phone and told her to come outside. She came to the door and the look on her face was priceless, "Did y'all buy it?" I shook my head no as I said, "Right now they're not talking my language. They want me to take it to Steve and let him look at it. They think he's an emotional buyer like eighty percent of the population," and I laughed uncontrollably at the thought. My husband was the most calculating and systematic person I knew. He is the type that has to sleep on a major purchase if the terms don't fit into his plans. It made life interesting to say the least. Our next stop was a drive through to get some lunch. It was after 2:00 and Jaida hadn't eaten since breakfast.

When we got to the shop, Steve came out and smiled at the sight of me commandeering such a massive vehicle. He walked up and opened my door. I got out and let him get behind the wheel and we drove around the block. I relayed my conversation with the sales manager and he confirmed what I already knew. At that time I didn't have any clients and no prospects for any of the existing inventory in the neighborhood I had been assigned. Our budget didn't have room for a car payment too far over $500 a month. I was already saying my farewells to the truck in my mind. When we got back to the shop one of the employees saw us drive up. He had come outside looking for Steve. When we got out so I could get back in the driver's seat the young man said, "Boss, that's your truck!" Steve threw himself across the hood and said, "I receive it in the name of Jesus!" We all laughed as he said, "If they still want $800 a month though they can keep it." I knew he was serious.

After I had my fun it was time to go back to the dealership. I went back to the shop to pick up Steve and we drove there in near silence. When we walked in the sales manager met us at the door. He shook Steve's hand, "So, what did you think?" Steve said, "Oh, it's nice, very nice." The manager showed us into his office. He sat down and said, "Are we going to be able to do business today?" Steve didn't crack a smile when he said, "That all depends on the price." We went through the same dance as we had earlier and the sales manager went to get his boss. When the dealership manager came into the office he gave us $625 a month as their final offer. Steve said, "Well, we can go home. That's not gonna work. Y'all have a nice day." The guy was flustered and he said, "Okay, I'll sell it to you for exactly what it cost me to pay it off at trade in, $25,000. That's my final offer." Steve said, "What kind of payment are we looking at?" The manager furrowed his brow and massaged his temple while he scrolled through screens on the computer and then he answered," $525 a month. That's all I can do."

Steve thought for a moment and asked me, "What are we paying now?" I said, "The van is $485 a month." Steve

thought some more and finally said, "Okay, we can do that."
We all shook hands and the finance guy came to get us so we
could sign the paperwork. While he was printing the loan
documents I told him the story of the poster over my desk.
He looked at Steve in disbelief, "You were gonna say no to
her dream car!?" Steve shrugged and said, "Hey, if the
numbers didn't add up. She already knew I would say no."
The finance guy shook his head and mumbled, "Man..."
We signed the papers, got the keys and went outside to
transfer our belongings to the Armada. It had been a long
but eventful day! I think getting that truck was the answer to
one of those forgotten prayers. Then again I had kept it
before my eyes and God's for two years.

One day I took a friend and her sisters to look at the house I
had dreamt about. While we were there we ran into the
owner. As it turned out we knew each other. My friend is
the type of person that will talk to anybody and often she
embarrasses us with her amazing gift of faith. She smiled
while telling the owner, "I think I know somebody that wants
to buy this house..." I grinned sheepishly and shrugged my
shoulders. The owner didn't respond so I didn't say anything
either. A few days later I got a call from his wife. She wanted
to know if Steve and I were really going to buy her house. I
explained that we had some credit issues preventing us from
buying a home right away but we did love the house. She was
persistent and even suggested I call the loan officer that they
used. They were pretty anxious to sell it. I agreed to try but I
got the same answer when I explained the situation to her
loan officer. We would have to wait two years and that was
still two months away. Not to mention, the price of that
house was more than we could manage.

There are times in life when we have to use wisdom and
common sense. We wanted a new home and we believed
God would make it happen for us. However, a $500,000
home wouldn't be a blessing if we couldn't even afford a fast

food dollar menu after we bought it. Proverbs 10:22 says, "The blessing of the Lord makes one rich and adds no sorrow with it." I would surely be crying if I couldn't enjoy life because I was chained to a half-million dollar albatross. I believed that we would get a house that didn't cost $500,000 but was well worth it. That's how it would be a blessing and make us rich at the same time.

After we realized our "dream" house wasn't attainable we started looking again in a lower price range. We settled on three choices that were in our budget and tried to narrow it down to one. The more I thought about it I couldn't see our family living in any one of our three choices. We talked it over some more and I decided to explore some other options. Steve took great joy in telling me; "I knew you wouldn't be happy until you got one built." I hated to admit it but he was right. This would soon prove to be a common occurrence during our home-building process. I looked at the model homes of several builders before I found one that met my approval. I found the name of that particular builder in MLS and I got up my nerve to call the office one morning. The office was closed that day but I left a detailed message.

When I got a call back, the builder seemed intrigued that I mentioned the house in question. I made an appointment and tried to wait patiently for the day to arrive. On the day of our meeting I saw God all over the place. The mortgage company I had already pre-qualified with was the builders' preferred lender. We discussed plans, exterior and interior materials. I thought the house we wanted would have to be built in a lower priced neighborhood but the builder really wanted to have something going near the model home I had looked at. The more concern I showed about the cost the more the builder reassured us that it wouldn't be a problem. So we got in the car and went to pick out a lot.

The builder even offered to have preliminary plans drawn up for free! We scheduled another appointment for a week later to come back and look at them. Again, God showed us favor. When all the details were agreed on all we had to do was put a small amount of money down to get started! I had been involved in the presale of a custom built home before and most builders ask for ten percent down. It was the first of many miracles. We visited our lot several times a week to watch the progress. We memorized the floor plan and took family and friends to look at our lot. We were like newlyweds buying their first home. Even though we had bought houses before, this time it felt like our first home. As the Bible says, "Any man that is in Christ is a new creature, old things have passed away, behold all things become new." (2 Corinthians 5:17)

4 A CHANGE IS GONNA COME

The new home market continued to perform poorly and I worried that I may have to switch companies again. My company only marketed new homes in three subdivisions. The subdivision I got my start subbing in had been virtually abandoned. The builders didn't help my broker pay for the advertising so costs had to be cut. The power was turned off in the construction trailer that served as our office. Two months later it was cleaned out and removed so we had to work out of the last house in the neighborhood that hadn't sold. I didn't mind but it felt like we would never sell that house. Lots of people came to look at it but we couldn't get an offer worked out. The builder was pressuring my broker and in turn that pressure trickled down to me.

Since I was now working real estate full time I had been assigned a neighborhood where I was the co-listing agent. I spent most of my time there because no matter what I did I couldn't get traffic into the subdivision that had the one house left. Finally we got an offer from an agent that said her buyers really wanted it. Unfortunately they were using a new loan program that I had never heard of before. There were many confusing steps in this loan they were using and even though an appraisal was ordered twice they could never close it. I think that is the moment when I gave up on selling that house. From that point I focused on my other neighborhood that had about seven houses for sale.

We didn't have much traffic in my neighborhood either but I worked hard to drive it in from every direction. We were in the back of an established neighborhood and we were in phase five of development. We didn't have any amenities; no clubhouse, no special features and no sparkle. There was nothing to help us compete with the comparable subdivisions in our price range. We had three builders but each had a different style. Two of them could build the same plan and I could walk in and tell immediately which one belonged to each builder. The first hint I got that the end was near was the people that seemed to be serial tire kickers. Some people came to the neighborhood every other weekend. They could tell me how long each house had been there. It was embarrassing.

Meanwhile, I got a call from the builder about the one lonely house in the abandoned subdivision. He asked when I had been out to check on it last. At the time my oldest son had a standing therapy appointment nearby every week so I took that opportunity to ride by the house and make sure everything was okay. But then I remembered we had cancelled the week before so it had been at least two weeks. Apparently a squatter had found the back door unlocked, presumably after that last appraisal, and as my mama says he "made himself to home". All the utilities were on so he had been able to use the built-in microwave, shower and even turn on the heat if he wanted. I was floored and the builder was irritated beyond words. I knew the builder was being courted by other agents to list the house and he was probably more convinced to switch now than ever.

I felt like a puppet in my neighborhood. One builder was luring customers by opening his houses four hours before we got there and putting out his own signs. Then he took potential buyers out to the suburbs so he could build them a house there. Another builder put his homes on a rental list with a different company and didn't mention it to me or my broker. I found out when the rental agent came out to show his houses to a potential tenant. I immediately called my broker and asked what was going on. It seemed like nobody knew anything. I had never even met the third builder. He only had one house for sale and it had been lived in briefly until the owners decided they wanted a custom built house. So he bought it back and built them what they wanted. Pretty soon, half our inventory was rented. In March only one of the four houses I managed to sell was in my subdivision. However, the appraisal came back much lower than we expected. To make the deal work my broker agreed to cut the commission but didn't tell me until the week before closing. Mad doesn't begin to describe how I felt. The builder broke even and to show his disgust he made rude comments, threw the keys on the table and stormed out of the closing after he signed all of his documents. I realized it was the end for me.

Since it was obvious I needed to find a resale company to

work for I called some of my friends and asked how they enjoyed the companies they were working for. I only had to talk to people at two companies in person to narrow it down after that. I was being heavily recruited by one company until I went to meet the owner and broker. After that conversation I knew that wasn't the place for me. Eventually I decided to go to an office that was part of a national franchise. Two other agents from my current office were already there and after meeting the broker and the owner I decided it was a good fit for me. My previous broker felt like we had all jumped ship together since we went to the same company but it wasn't about that. I just wanted out of new construction so I could learn the resale side and hone my skills. It was clear we were entering a market similar to the one in the eighties, minus double digit interest rates, and only the strong would survive.

By this time our house was coming along nicely. Our foundation was done on April 19th and after we got through a rainy spell, construction on our house took off. In eleven days' time it was completely framed, closed in, windows had been installed and the shingles were on. Nobody believed us when they looked at the pictures. God was truly pouring out a blessing from the windows of heaven. Our builder was working hard to get us in before school started, checking the progress almost daily. Once we got into the fine details I could see God's hand in each decision that was made. Originally, I picked a dark gold brick because it looked similar to mortar-wash. I knew that mortar-wash was too expensive so I didn't even ask. I wanted to be respectful of the budget our builder was working from. Once the time came to order bricks the gold brick was unavailable and we got a call to come in and look at an alternative. I was overcome with happiness when I saw the brick that I was getting. It was exactly what I originally wanted but didn't ask for because of the price. God was giving me the desires of my heart. (Psalm 37:4)

Many times, God wanted to see if I really trusted Him. When we met to finalize the plans I saw that we would have two doorways on either side of the pass-through over the kitchen sink. I thought to myself, 'I sure would like to make all three of those openings arched'. I didn't say a word to the builder because God said, "Will you trust me?" When we went back to look at the final plans the openings had all been arched. That is how God works when He has placed divine favor on your life and you trust Him to handle all the details. Just like the change with the bricks, we got several surprises when we met to discuss the placement of cable, electrical and phone outlets. The rough plumbing had been done and we met the rep for the company that would be fabricating our bathroom countertops, jetted tub and shower surround. When we got to the kitchen our builder informed us that we would have a stained wood cathedral-style ceiling in our breakfast room just like in the model home. I was so shocked I didn't know what to say. I'm not sure if the builder even realized why we were getting so many upgrades. The bible says God holds the heart of the king in His hand. (Proverbs 21:1)

The week after that we met again to pick out cabinets, granite countertops, ceramic tile, carpet and wood flooring. I had taken the entire weekend to decide on paint colors. We got yet another surprise when we learned the cabinets wouldn't be the ordinary honey maple we started with. We were getting a chocolate glaze because the builder wanted the kitchen to look nice and be suitable for a successful resale. Prior to that, I really wanted the glaze but I knew it would go over the budget we had to work with. God stepped right in and took care of that. When we got to the flooring store it took less than twenty minutes to choose everything.

We were getting top-quality tile for the kitchen that was left over from a house that was built for the Parade of Homes. The tile we chose for the master bath as well as the children's bathrooms was equally beautiful. The hardwood flooring was the one thing that left me shaking my head in disbelief. In my ideal house the floors were real hand-shaven wood. They had a beautiful ripple effect when the light hit them. Our budget would only allow for a laminate floor and with three active children it would be more practical. I took one look at the samples we had to pick from and all three of us locked in on the same piece simultaneously. It was laminate but it looked like real wood. To top it off it even had the ripple effect like hand-shaved flooring.

A couple of weeks after that the bricks went up. We went to inspect the progress at the end of the first day of brickwork. We were getting a French provincial brick with a light grayish-taupe color. Due to the texture and finish on the bricks they couldn't be scraped off so the mortar had to be leveled off evenly, creating a look similar to mortar-wash. They were more beautiful than I had imagined. With the dark brown vinyl siding we were using for the trim, I would have my Old World villa when it was all finished. By the second week of June we had all bricks, insulation and some sheet rock. Steve estimated the sheet rock would be completely installed by the end of that week.

Months earlier, after we picked our lot we had taken my godparents to see it. On that day we stood on the land and prayed. We asked God to show us favor in all aspects of building our home. When we went to pick out furniture, the prices and my taste didn't mix very well. I found bedroom furniture for Julian but not much else. On the day before my birthday we took a trip to a furniture store about an hour away. I took my famous binder with all the pictures and fabric samples. We went with the intention of getting prices on the master bedroom furniture and something for Jarod's bedroom.

Once we saw what was available and showed our salesperson

the pictures, we got Jarod's furniture, a dining room table with six chairs and a loveseat and sofa for the great room. We saved about $1,900! The dining room furniture was a special treat. I saw the same set at a store a year before but didn't have the money to buy it. Thinking I would never be able to get it again I started looking for alternatives but never found anything that I liked as much. What made the deal even sweeter was that the price was almost $1,000 less. God can and will give us the desires of our hearts if we trust Him. We must trust Him in the small things as well as the big things.

By the third week of June the sheet rock was being finished and the lighting store was putting some samples together for us to choose from. Our cabinets had been delivered but we still had about a week before they could be installed. Our builder was shocked when they opened the cabinet boxes and they were the wrong style. After thinking about it, the original style I had chosen would not have been as pretty. We agreed to keep them and continued to watch the progress. I managed to limit my visits to once or twice a week. I loved watching the framing but the tedious parts of the building process didn't hold my interest. I was ready to see cabinets going in and paint on the walls.

One day while I was at the dentist's office with my sons when my dad called. I couldn't really talk so I let it go to voicemail. By the time we were done I knew he was at work so I made a mental note to call him back the next day. Well, things happened and I forgot. Two days later I was on the interstate headed to a continuing education class when my brother called. He said Dad had been rushed to the hospital and he was on his way to see what was going on. I asked if he knew what happened. He said Dad had been at home talking to a friend that stopped by. Suddenly he had slumped over and his friend called 911. I told him to call as soon as he knew anything. I was in the middle of the interstate and the hospital he was being transported to was twenty minutes in the opposite direction. I didn't know what to do so I just prayed and asked God to be with him but deep down I knew he was already gone. I asked God to take Dad into his arms and to comfort my brother.

That's when I remembered my prayer for Dad that God had answered two years prior. My dad was a complicated man and life had been difficult for him at times. After serving in the Vietnam War he came home carrying more baggage than he left with from a mental perspective. He was tormented by the flashbacks and shattered dreams so he self-medicated to cope. He had been diagnosed with prostate cancer in 2006 and his doctor recommended surgery. He wasn't completely honest with the medical personnel about how often he indulged in certain habits and after surgery he had a strange reaction to all the medicines they gave him. Then they pumped him full of sedatives that only compounded the problem. The result was a hospitalization that lasted eleven days. When Dad finally got out he said his hospital stay had been worse than the time he spent in Vietnam.

Before he was discharged and it looked like he may not leave anytime soon, I went to see him the one and only time of his whole stay. You can never be prepared to see a parent in a vulnerable state no matter how sick they've been. Just as I had done when my mom had open heart surgery fourteen years prior I wept at the sight of my daddy. After I had cried and prayed quietly for a few minutes I got up and stood next to his bed. I asked him if he knew who I was. When other people had visited he had either called them by the wrong name or not recognized them at all. He said he knew me and I asked him if he remembered taking me and my brother to air shows on the military base when we were kids. He whispered, "Yeah…" He looked at me like it was all coming back to him. Before I left I anointed his head and hands with some blessed oil. I laid my hand on his head and prayed that

God would guide the doctors and nurses in the best way to care for him. I told God I wasn't ready to let him go. He slipped off into a fitful sleep from the sedatives and I left. The next day my brother called and said he had made great improvements.

As I drove I realized God had kept up his end of the deal but now it was time for Daddy to go home. Although I couldn't prove it I had peace that he was with our heavenly Father. I got to the office where my CE class was being held. I didn't know what else to do so I went in and sat down just before the class started. I remember feeling frozen with dread of the reality I was about to face. About an hour into the class we took a break and my brother texted me that he had made it to the hospital and the doctors had done all they could but Dad was gone. I suddenly had trouble thinking clearly. I read the words but they didn't sink in for about five minutes. Then the tears started and people crowded around me in the hallway. The instructor was the same one I had taken my real estate courses with and he assured me I could make up the CE class. I got my things and left.

I sat in my car for a few minutes to compose myself before I drove off. I called Steve and told him what happened and he said he was going to leave work as soon as he could to come home. I had dropped Jaida off at the beauty salon so I went to pick her up. When I walked in with sunglasses on my stylist immediately knew something was wrong. She was also my sister in Christ and we knew each other well. I had left the car running since it was so hot and I shooed Jaida out to wait on me. When she was out of earshot I choked out the news to my stylist and she put her arm around me and led me to her break room. Another stylist followed and I told her what had happened. Those two women of God prayed for me and I got the strength to go home. On the way I explained to Jaida that Granddaddy was in heaven. All she said was, "Do the boys know this?" I said, "No, not yet."

She turned to stare out the window and I was grateful for the silence.

My mom had been at my house with the boys and when I walked in she was calm but I knew she was sad. Even though my parents were divorced they eventually became good friends again after my mom's bypass surgery. They loved to laugh about the things my kids did and they both spoiled them rotten. I knew Dad's death would be difficult for her. When Steve got home my mom got out of there as fast as she could. I knew she wanted to be alone to grieve in her own way. Steve and I went to our bedroom and he sat on the bed with me while I told him what details I had. The tears wouldn't stop so he finally tucked me into bed and turned out the lights. I just wanted to go to sleep and hope the awful truth wouldn't be there when I woke up. The next few days were rough to say the least.

My brother, Chris, was willing to handle the arrangements and I was more than happy to let him. I was in no shape to make any major decisions. We went to the funeral home and the cemetery together and after that I had to go home and get into bed again. I left all of the other details up to my brother and my sister-in-law. They put together a lovely program and my sister-in-law, Diana, found a pianist for us. Her father officiated and he asked my pastor to do a New Testament scripture reading. The only request I made for the service was a few minutes to speak. My brother didn't want dozens of people getting up to do reflections but he allowed me and one of my dad's friends from high school and college to say something. I told the story of Dad's hospital stay after prostate surgery and how I had asked God for more time with him. I thanked and praised God for the two years he gave us and I took my seat. The entire chapel was clapping and praising God with me. I was just glad I made it through without being overcome with emotion.

When I was little I had been a daddy's girl. After my parents' divorce I had felt caught in the middle but ultimately gave up on being the peacemaker. Dad and I had grown apart during my teenage years and early adulthood. Once I had kids of my own and rededicated my life to Christ I decided to make the best of it. You only get one set of parents and life is too short to dwell on the mistakes they made. God knows I had made some mistakes as a parent too. Children don't come with instruction manuals but when you know better only then can you do better. I had once read a quote from Dr. Maya Angelou that said something like, "It doesn't matter what kind of relationship you had with your parents. When they die you will miss them." She was so right. I mourned for about six months and even now I still have my moments. My birthday is in the same month that Dad passed. His birthday in February is sometimes difficult. Thanksgiving and Christmas are no exception either but God is still good.

The proof that God can make something good happen in the midst of a sad situation unfolded before my eyes just before my dad's funeral. We were building a house but we had no idea where we would get the money to close with once it was finished. We were contacted by the human resource department from my dad's employer and we found out he had a retirement fund. I think he would have been pleased to know that he contributed to our dream house in a way none of us expected. I only sold two more houses that year so we needed every penny of that money to help pay our bills.

5 PRESSING IN

By July 2, we had paint on the walls and crown molding was due to be installed the next day along with the stone on the front of the house. The vinyl siding and vinyl cedar shake shingles were on and it all looked fabulous. We had to make a few changes from the original paint colors that we picked but I loved it once it was done. That same day all of the interior doors had been delivered and were waiting in the kitchen. They would be installed and then the painter would take them down to be painted. The whole process seemed backwards to me.

On July 12, we went to see what was being done and found all the cabinetry installed and hardware being put on. The crown molding and trim had been completed except around the temporary entry doors and the unfinished staircase. It was the most detailed crown molding I had ever seen. The cabinet hardware was beautiful and we were so elated about every little detail. By July 23, we had tile started in the kitchen and the tile in all of the bathrooms was done. All it needed was grout, which would probably be done the next day. The tubs in the kids' bathrooms had been finished with marble edging. All the doors had been prepped for paint. It was so exciting!

Our builder had already ordered the front door and the company that would be installing the stairs was ready to get started. The builder added a special threshold pattern in the tile at each doorway. The tile in the laundry room and half bath was laid on a diagonal. The granite was on order and we were anxiously waiting to see the whole kitchen come together. I had so many emotions going through me. This would be the first time we had owned and lived in our own home in almost seven years. To me, this was the last step to our new beginning as a couple. God does things in His own way but He is always on time.

On July 28, I registered the children for school with no problem. Since we had not closed on the house yet, I didn't have proof of residence. However, God is faithful and after I prayed about it, I knew it would be okay. As it turned out, the wife of one of my dad's good friends worked in the office at the middle school. Then there was the sweetest lady in the office of the elementary school. She accepted the paperwork I had because she didn't want the boys to miss any days of school. I was overjoyed to learn that school started on the eleventh and not the sixth like I originally thought. Putting our new address on all the paperwork was so surreal. We rode by the new house afterwards and the garage door was going up. The kids were finally starting to get excited too.

On July 30, the lighting supplier got tired of my polite but persistent phone calls. They finally got the builder's approval to let me come in and look at what the consultant had picked out. I couldn't believe my eyes when I saw the samples. Every one of them was perfect! I did make one change on the fixtures for the stairwell. Instead of a lantern style fixture, I preferred a flush mount sconce. I didn't want to give the boys anything else to swing from. Even the doorbell was pretty! What was even more surprising was the striking resemblance of my fixtures to the ones in my former ideal house. To my knowledge, the consultant never saw that house so I know God picked out my lights just for me!

After we left the lighting store we drove by the house. The electricians had installed all of the wiring for the HVAC units and the breaker box was up. All they were waiting for was the power company to come out and hook the power to the breaker box. Once that was done the electrical finish work could be completed. I was hoping we would make it in by the third week in August. A few days later, we went up and were shocked to see the granite counter tops and kitchen sink installed. The plumber was there working on the jetted tub. I was thrilled! The only thing to top that was driving to Calera, AL, the next day to pick up our furniture.

August 11th was the first day of school. After we picked up the kids we went by our house. The landscape and irrigation company was installing the sprinkler system and getting ready to put the plants in. The stairs were done and all the railings and treads were in place. Almost all of the lights were up and the appliances had been delivered. The builder had kept another surprise from me. We ended up getting a two-story mantel after all. Most of the electrical work had been finished as well. It was all coming together nicely.

Soon, we discovered that the wrong cook top had been ordered and the exhaust hood was the wrong color. This meant more delays and that was obviously beyond our control. Since we understood that everything was happening in God's timing, we continued doing what we knew how to do. We praised God for his goodness because if He allowed these delays, there was a reason. He would have our house finished when the time was right. Psalm 127:1 says, "Unless the Lord builds the house, its builder labors in vain…"

On the bright side, the painter was finishing up and the electrician worked on the rest of the lights. The landscapers rolled out the sod and placed the plants in their positions around the front of the house. The sprinkler system was completed and tested. The exterior was almost done except for the shutters and permanent doors. All that was left was the flooring and plumbing. The last time we went by the house it was 3:00 on a Friday afternoon. To our surprise we went the following Sunday and discovered a driveway, completed sod and all the shrubs had been planted. Before we left, the landscaper showed up to turn on the sprinklers. We were so happy to finally see a driveway.

On Wednesday, August 20, I went to see what was going on. Steve had already informed me that the hardwood flooring had been delivered and was waiting in the laundry room. The painters were finishing the second floor foyer area and working their way up the hall. They had already finished the great room and dining room. The plumber was upstairs installing the tub and sink faucets. All the faucets had been installed on the first floor including my long-awaited pot filler! The two-story mantel had been painted and put back in place. The shutters had been hung the day before and they made the house stand out even more. Everything was gorgeous; we were getting more anxious to move by the day.

By August 25, the kids were starting the third week of school and the house was winding up nicely. The trim was being completed on the stairs and in the rooms with tile and wood flooring. The electricity was on in all parts of the house. The doorknobs were all installed and the towel bars were up in every bathroom. All we needed was carpet, heat pumps and the permanent doors. The weather was causing a slight delay since hurricanes kept blowing through the gulf and sending lots of rain our way. I tried not to obsess about it and occupied myself with finding the perfect wrought iron piece to go inside the second section of our mantel. One day I stopped at Hobby Lobby even though it was storming. They were having a half-price sale on all wall décor and I got the piece I wanted for my two story mantel. I could have clicked my heels with joy.

By the end of that week, we had our closing date. We were scheduled to close on Friday, September 5, 2008 at 8:15 in the morning. So much had changed in the mortgage industry while we were building that the lender requested we bring money to closing. Even with our builder paying a large portion of the closing costs they still wanted just over 1% from us at closing. I was reminded of the promises God made to us about our new home. God said His blessings come without sorrow, and that is the word we agreed on when we started looking for a house. He also promised us that everything we took to our new house would be new. We had trusted God to bring us this far and we knew He would bring us through the closing victoriously.

When God promises you something, His word has to be tried and tested, Psalm 18:30 and Proverbs 30:5 verify this. I knew that God would get the glory out of this situation and we decided to continue on with preparations to move. I will admit that I got distracted for a moment but I realized that if God would allow them to make us pay something at closing, He had a bigger blessing in store for us. We were less than a week away from getting our blessing so there had to be some opposition.

Our walk-through was scheduled for the day before closing. Steve asked me to call the builder to get permission to store some things in the garage of our new house. When I got there for the walk-through he had moved half our belongings in already. Our bed was in the master bedroom and some of the other furniture that had been in storage was set up. We went home after that to pack the final boxes. As we were discussing what to take on the last trip of the day my cell phone rang and it was our loan officer. She was calling to say the closing would not happen the next morning; it may be later in the afternoon instead. We went ahead and made one last trip to the new house that night. When we went back to the old house I had trouble getting to sleep. Worry kept trying to creep into my thoughts.

On Friday morning we got up and went ahead with our plans. We waited for the phone to ring with the time of our closing. Finally at 3:00 our loan officer called to say there would be no closing that day. I was deflated and Steve was unmoved. He continued moving and arranging furniture and acting as if nothing had changed. In both our hearts we heard God say, "Possess the land." (Deut 1:8) Almost another week went by with many more changes. The bank that financed the construction loan had figured out we were living in the house and they pressured our builder about closing. We finally closed on Thursday, September 11, 2008. The number eleven is significant for disorder and that is certainly what we had. However, God is faithful and He never took back our blessing. We simply had to stand on the word He gave us, get into agreement with each other and believe.

We wanted to invite our friends and family over for a housewarming and our church family helped us organize it. In late October we had the party and about eighty people came through our house that day. It was a powerful moment in our lives to show everybody what God had done for us. He had taken a simple dream and created something tangible that couldn't be denied. As 2008 drew to a close we were optimistic about the future. I have since learned that whenever you experience a major move of God that took you to the top of the mountain, you can expect a valley right around the corner.

In spite of transferring to a new company my business was still floundering. I got some referrals from friends and past clients but not all of them resulted in a sale. I was still fairly new in the business and I didn't have a large past client database to call on. God was still faithful and we even took our first real family vacation to Orlando that summer. A little research on the Internet and some resourcefulness on my part got us a week in a timeshare for a tiny fraction of what it would have cost to stay in a cheap hotel. We went to Universal Studios and had a marvelous time. But by the end of 2009 we told the kids we all had to make some sacrifices. I involved them in it and taught them how to save money and compare prices. They each got money from their grandparents when they did well on their report cards. I showed them how to make wise choices about how they spent it. I had to make my trips to the office or any other place in the city count. I couldn't afford to drive all over town where ever I wanted anymore.

I worked hard to convert every lead I got but it seemed like every time I got close to sealing a deal it did a complete 180. There were several more things that happened that almost sucked the joy out of me before that year was over. I was out showing houses one day when I drove past the street some of my friends lived on. I got to the stop sign in front of their street and when I glanced over towards their house there was a for sale sign in their yard. I understand business is business but they had purposefully kept it a secret from me. I would have felt better if they had come to me and simply said they listed with someone else. The thing that broke my heart the most was when I tried to help another couple I knew well. They came to me and asked about buying a house. I told them the process and they got to work on it with a loan officer I sent them to. It was going to take several months but they said they would come back to me when they were ready.

After some time passed the wife called one day and said they were ready to go. I was ecstatic. Then she told me they had already found the house they wanted but it was for sale by owner. The owner told them he couldn't afford to pay an agent's commission. He also said that if he had to involve an agent he would have to drastically increase the price of the house. Obviously, they didn't want to pay more for the house. I was curious as to why she had called me. The answer to my question was they had hoped I would write the contract for them. After I regained my composure I explained that I could give them suggestions but if I participated in the sale my brokerage had to be compensated. I told them what they needed to do and they thanked me. I was so hurt it took all I had to function for a week afterwards. When they had their housewarming I could barely afford to buy them a card from the dollar store. But I went and smiled bravely as she gave me a tour of their new home and talked about how our story had inspired them. I was trying hard to be happy for them. We ended up leaving before the food was served because I just couldn't take it anymore.

With no prospects for a sale in the near future I started working on my resume. I got a friend who was a former Realtor to help me. She had transitioned into pharmaceutical sales and I thought I wanted to try that too. She even tried to get me her old job in outside sales. I had a phone interview but never made it to the next phase. I was crushed. We were barely making ends meet and the holidays were coming. I fell into a deep depression. Most days I stayed at home and even in bed, crying or staring blankly at the walls. I only shared our situation with certain people. If I had gone to some of the people we knew they would have said it was foolish of us to build a home. There were a lot of people that had wanted me to keep my full time job but they didn't understand that wasn't an option. I didn't know that the same faith I had to build the house would have to be doubled in order for us to keep it.

Steve didn't seem phased by the facts. I was the one that couldn't sleep and cried all the time. Steve's parents and his grandmother gave us money to get the kids gifts for Christmas. I was both thankful and humbled. We thought 2010 surely had to be better than 2009. In late February we got a letter saying our mortgage had been purchased by a major banking firm that spanned sixteen states. They were not as forgiving as our previous mortgage company. The old bank didn't call unless we missed a payment. The new bank started calling on the sixteenth if they hadn't been paid. Then the letters started with threats of foreclosure if we didn't pay all the back fees and get our account current in thirty days. I called a friend and asked about refinancing but we were upside down according to her company's standards and the current property values. When we got our tax return we got caught up on our payments for a while.

By the end of March I was feeling the urge to change companies again. I talked to my broker and told him the situation we were in with our home. He offered to help me as much as he could. I felt a little better for a few days but the urge was back by the next week. In the meantime another agent called me to schedule an appointment for one of my listings. We were already connected on a social media site so we chatted for a few minutes. She asked me how things were going and I'm one of those people that can't really lie well. I vented my frustration about the things that had been bothering me and she encouraged me. Then she asked if I had ever considered working for her company. I told her I was looking for a change and I even knew her broker personally. He had coached my son in little league a few years back. I went to the office to meet with him and I knew it was where I should have been a long time ago.

Being a part of the new company was amazing! Some of the costs I had struggled to pay on my own were taken care of for us. Our sales meetings were informative and our broker made sure we were aware of every change in the industry. Almost immediately after I switched over some of my listings went under contract. May was the best month I'd had in a very long time. June was great too but the best surprise came in July. I had worked my tail off to close two sales and I had two more pending. A couple of clients that were having trouble accepting the changing market had given me a hard time. I was sick of being abused for factors beyond my control; namely inferior product and areas of town where growth was stagnant. I went to the first sales meeting in August thinking if I could just make it through I was going to clean out my desk afterwards. I planned to go home and lick my wounds. Right before the meeting was over our broker pulled out the awards for July. I had long since stopped expecting to hear my name. A handful of top producers at my last company always got those. In two years I only won one award there. I almost fell off my chair when my broker called my name for Top Sales Agent of the month! It was one of the best days in my career.

6 ALL IN A DAY'S WORK

I've had so many unforgettable moments and clients over my short career. One time I had showings scheduled when I was fasting yet again. Fasting is something you have to prepare for and in those days my preparation was less than average. I was due to show houses in the next county and I didn't have time to stop and eat some veggies. This was one of those times my whole family was with me as well. I went to a local fast food burger chain to get us all something to eat. I couldn't drive and eat a salad and Steve didn't know where we were going. I ordered a veggie burger and hoped for the best. I have a long history of having an extremely sensitive stomach so I should have known better.

The young couple and her parents were meeting us at the restaurant since it was near the road we were taking to get to the area they wanted to live in. We got on the road with them following me in their car. About half way there I started to feel really sick to my stomach. "Oh Lord," I thought, "That veggie burger may not have been the best idea..." By the time we got to the first house I got out of the car and I almost doubled over. The sun was beaming down on me and beads of sweat popped out all over my face. My stomach was in knots and each step was excruciating. I was terrified that I might have an accident and the closest public restroom was miles away. Most of the houses we were looking at didn't have working plumbing yet. I had to pray the prayer of faith because we had several houses to look at.

I didn't know if it was the fact that I had printed my data sheets in black and white or the sun beaming down on me but all the garden homes started to look alike. The ones that were still under construction didn't have address numbers on them so I was even more confused. The couple chatted with the parents and I fumbled with lockboxes and keys for over an hour. Then we went inside one house that I later discovered hadn't been on my list. We walked in to find it was professionally staged and my buyers were instantly in love. The builder had added many upgrades and the workmanship was impeccable. The floor plan was unlike any other we had viewed that day. They walked through it over and over and I sat down on the leather sofa trying not to make any sudden movements so I wouldn't implode.

Finally it was unanimous and this was the house they wanted. Then one of the buyers picked up a flyer off the table and we discovered the house was about $15,000 more than they wanted to spend. We negotiated the price down to where they could manage it and we got the ball rolling after the seller accepted. They chose to do a home inspection even though the house was brand new because it had been sitting for several months. It was a smart move because we discovered that part of the heat pump wasn't working and neither was the jetted tub. Another twist to the story was the lender requiring a ten year home warranty because the house was outside the city limits. We didn't find out about that until two days before closing and it almost killed the deal. The owner of the company I worked for at the time went to bat for me and got the listing company to split the cost of the warranty. We did our walk-through the next day and it went well; everything had been fixed or corrected from our inspection. There were only a few spots that needed touch up paint but overall we were good to go. Closing day was fun and the parents came back for the occasion.

I had one set of clients that nearly gave me an ulcer by the time I sold their house and negotiated the purchase of the new one. They had found their dream house one day while out riding around through a random neighborhood. Before we went to take a look at it I did my usual research. The house had been listed for quite some time and the price had dropped steadily over the months it sat on the market. The couple had already begun a few projects on their current home to get it ready for the market. They seemed optimistic that the house would still be waiting when they were ready. We listed it a few months later. This couple had several friends and they didn't want any of them to know they were selling their house. At one point, the husband even contemplated not having a sign in the yard. I explained that the sign was a huge factor in getting showings. Many times an agent may be driving a buyer to a showing, see your sign and decide to stop. About a month later, that was exactly how it happened.

Once we got an accepted offer on their home we wrote an offer on the house they wanted. Unfortunately, there was another party that wanted the house and their offer was accepted over ours. My clients were a little disappointed but I suggested we look at backups while we waited to see if the other offer worked out. The wife was determined that this was their house and she wouldn't look at other houses. Her husband met me to look at a couple but we never found one quite like the original. A week or so went by and the wife called me to say the house they wanted was still active. I called the listing agent to inquire about the status and he wouldn't return my calls. My client got someone else to call the other agent and ask about the house. Imagine our surprise when he told her, "Well, I had an offer but it didn't work out." I called him right away.

The other agent stressed that our last offer had been too low and he gave away a critical piece of information without meaning to. He said, "This guy won't entertain an offer below _____." So we made our initial offer for that amount. After all, he told me out of his own mouth what the bottom line was. Before it was over I had morphed into a pit bull in a skirt. I had my clients pushing me on one end and Mr. Old Money broker barking at me on the other. My broker at the time was recovering from surgery so I couldn't call or get much help from someone on pain medication. I decided to put on my big girl knickers and deal with it. I negotiated for my buyers and got the price they wanted, a home warranty and an allowance for repairs! After that Mr. Old Money kept calling me saying, "Now, you're sure their home is gonna close?" I had to tell him 'yes' at least three times a week until he was confident there wouldn't be a problem.

My clients had already completed all of their repairs and our closing for their current home was a done deal. We had a tricky situation when it came to their moving date. The buyer for their home agreed to give them until the weekend after our closing. I explained this to Mr. Old Money a dozen times. We were down to the wire and he finally admitted in a roundabout way that he didn't think my people would be able to buy the house so he didn't tell his seller until the Tuesday before we were supposed to close. The seller lived over 1,000 miles away and now he wasn't sure he could get a flight out to make it to the closing. I was furious! Mr. Old Money wanted me to ask if we could push the closing back a day or so. I told him I would call my people and ask but he should expect the answer to be no. Sure enough I called the wife at work and leaving out the drama-laden details I simply asked if they would be willing to close a day later. Just as I suspected, the answer was an emphatic no. I called Mr. Old Money back and told him to get his client on the red eye if he had to or get a power of attorney but we were closing on the day the contract specified.

The closing of my clients' current home went off without a hitch. Unfortunately the other agent didn't know how to put her cell phone on vibrate or she just chose not to. She took at least half a dozen calls at the table while the attorney was trying to explain the loan documents to *her* client. I had never seen anything like it before in my life. I wanted to say, "If you don't put that phone on vibrate I'm gonna take it and you might get it back when this is over!" She seemed totally oblivious that her behavior was less than acceptable. My clients kept looking at me with smirks on their faces and I just bit my lip. If we had been in a CE class she would have turned it off to avoid a steep fine.

Of course we couldn't have a smooth closing for the new house after all of this had transpired. We got to the closing early only to discover the seller and Mr. Old Money were still in route. We sat in the conference room at a huge table and waited. They finally showed up and I could see why so many little maintenance items had been neglected in the house. The seller chatted with us and we found out he was a professor. He certainly looked more bookish than do-it-yourself. I could imagine him burying his nose in a thick tome like War and Peace every weekend instead of painting the guest room or fixing the leaky sink. Overall the home inspection hadn't shown anything major but there were enough little items to add up to two months' worth of weekend projects.

The bank was taking their sweet time putting the money into the attorney's escrow account. We had to sit at the table and make small talk for another thirty minutes before we could leave. Finally my clients got their keys and I had my company's check in my hand. I went back to the old house with them to get my lockbox off the door. We were standing in the kitchen and the husband got very serious. He turned to me and said, "Through this whole process we never could tell if you were stressed or upset. Your demeanor never changed and neither did the tone of your voice." I told him that I been stressed plenty of days but I was taught to never let people see you sweat. We laughed about the day's events and I thanked God the whole ordeal was over.

Sometime later I had another near ulcer experience. I listed a house for a couple that I knew through mutual friends. When I met Sandra for the first time our friend, Gloria, had called me about showing them a house on their lunch break. I met them at the house the next day and it was a foreclosure that was in good shape. It needed a few things like paint and carpet but it was livable. Sandra liked it but it wasn't everything she had hoped for. Over the course of the next few weeks this pattern repeated itself. Gloria would call me and say, "Sandra wants to look at another house!" I would meet them and Sandra would be slightly disappointed after seeing it in person. Finally I started emailing Sandra some homes that I thought she might like. She liked one that I sent and we met again so she could see it. This time from the moment Sandra walked through the door all she could say was, "Oooooh!"

Now the only problem we had was getting her husband to come and look at it. I thought he was always working long hours at his job. I soon found out that Sandra hadn't even told her husband what she was planning. Sandra was finally able to get her husband to come under false pretenses. She told him she wanted to ride around and explore the area where the house was located. She had made it seem like it was a totally random thing. When Sandra's husband George walked into the house, where I had been waiting for almost an hour, he knew something was going on. I realized that George felt he had walked into a set up. I showed him all the features of the house but he grew more indifferent by the minute. Sandra on the other hand kept touching everything in the house like a little kid.

As we were leaving George asked me about the rental sign that was in the front yard next to the for sale sign. I told him the house had been on the market for a while and the owners probably wanted relief. They had already moved on but the house payment still needed to be made. If they couldn't sell it a tenant would help relieve the constant strain of paying for two homes. As we were walking out the front door another family had driven up and run up the front steps. I asked if they were meeting their agent. The wife tried to slide past me into the house so swiftly that I almost closed the door on her. She was talking fast, "Well, we were just driving by and we saw it open so we thought we would take a look." I must have 'sucker' tattooed on my forehead. I reluctantly let them in but I followed them like a hawk. I said, "We have other appointments so we need to get going…" "Oh, we'll be quick," the wife said. They asked me some questions and I gave them my card. A week later the signs were gone and someone had moved in. When I checked MLS it said the house had been rented.

I broke the news to Sandra and she was unhappy about it. We talked about building but I told her we needed to get their house sold first. We set up an appointment for me to come over and look at it a few days later. When I met with her and George he was as hostile as ever. He seemed very opposed to paying any of the buyer's closing costs, which is almost customary in this part of the country. He also didn't want to provide a home warranty. That's when I put my foot in my mouth and told him if it came down to making the deal work I would pay for it. I was counting on selling their home and then helping them buy or build a new one. George had kept the house in almost new condition and Sandra kept the interior spotless. All I needed to do was come back and take pictures after we did the listing paperwork that night.

George wanted a pretty high price for his home and with the comps (or recent comparable sales) available I wasn't sure he would get it. We didn't get as many showings as I had hoped and I was sure the price had something to do with it. I emailed Sandra some lots that were available near the house that had gotten away. I didn't know it then but there were many lots for sale that weren't listed in MLS or even had signs on them. I tried to get George and Sandra to consider my builder but I think George would have run naked down the interstate in rush hour traffic before he let me be part of the next house. I concentrated on getting their house sold while I made another rookie mistake. I didn't ask them to sign an exclusive buyer's agent agreement so I could represent them in the purchase of their next home. I just assumed they would let me help them. My mistake would haunt me for a long time after that.

Unbeknownst to me George talked to someone that had a contractor's license. This person knew a broker that owned some unlisted lots for sale in the area Sandra wanted. They talked to the other broker and signed a lot reservation form without my knowledge. By the time we got an offer on their house I was two steps behind. I worked hard to make the deal work and yes I ended up paying for the home warranty. I felt so stupid but I didn't know what else to do. I had to keep my word. Sandra completely backed out of the negotiation process. When I read George the details of the contract over the phone he exploded when I got to the closing date. I told him over and over that we could require as many days as they wanted to move out. Another option was to close on a later date. I'm sure he was stressed because they hadn't found temporary housing to live in while the new house was being built. But since I wasn't his buyer's agent I couldn't really help him with that now.

The buyer was a little odd and she had to consult her mother for everything. A few days before closing Sandra told me they both had showed up on her doorstep in the middle of a weekend morning to measure for curtains! Personally, I wouldn't have let them in without an appointment. There was more drama at the closing. The buyer wanted several family members to attend the closing but they lived out of town. I tried to reschedule the time but Sandra and George were leaving town that afternoon. We went in early to sign their documents and the buyer came later. It was probably a blessing in disguise. I found George and Sandra after their house was built and I still sent them cards but I didn't expect any referrals.

My first few years in the business taught me a lot. I soon learned why the seasoned agents rolled their eyes and sighed dramatically when telling stories of closings that went haywire. It can literally drive you insane. Sometimes you can catch it before it goes too far and sometimes you have to pray and hope for the best. When I was working in my new subdivision there was a house on a corner lot in the second phase of the neighborhood that was for sale by owner. It had been empty as long as I could remember and the history in MLS showed several listings. One day the owner, Mr. Thomas, called me and asked me about listing it. He said he felt I may be more successful since I worked in the neighborhood every day. They had moved twelve hundred miles away and his daughter, who was attending college nearby, wasn't always available to show the house. I didn't think it was a good idea for a young woman to go alone to show a vacant house anyway. Realtors are trained to handle things like that. We arranged a viewing and Mrs. Thomas was in town so she met me and gave me a tour. I saw the biggest problem right away.

The house sat on the lot in such a way that it never got full sun. The windows had heavy treatments and blinds. This meant the sun was blocked out even at daybreak. This would make it difficult to get good pictures and what I saw in MLS proved my hypothesis. They had many upgrades in the house but without a powerful flash and all the windows open you'd never notice. It would be one dark, uninteresting picture after another. The yard was fully fenced and the corner lot was meticulously manicured. I later discovered Mrs. Thomas was an avid gardener. I called Mr. Thomas after I looked at the house and I told him I would list it. I emailed him the paperwork the next morning and he sent it back right away. With the price I helped him choose from the recent sales of existing homes it was only a matter of time. Since I had full access to the house I took pictures at various times of day to get the best shots.

Just as I predicted, it only took sixty days to get the house under contract. The agent that brought the offer was a thorn in my flesh. She was a fellow rookie but from her approach I knew what company she worked for immediately. She bad-mouthed the house and named every one of its worst features. I assumed she did that to make me convince my people they should take any offer we got. She went on about the house not having gra-nite counters, as if granite rhymed with mesquite. Yes, it was dusty but it had been closed up for several months. And yes my sellers were aware the kitchen floor was dirty. Sheesh, did she think Hazel or Alice lived there? She gave me the "There is so much competition" speech because of closely priced new homes right around the corner. I reminded her that those new homes didn't have granite and none of them had full privacy fences. Plus my listing had a screened back porch. She took the hint that I wasn't giving away any information so she said she would talk to her clients and get back to me.

When the offer came in it was full of all sorts of requests. They wanted a flooring allowance because they claimed the floors were in such bad shape. They also wanted money to upgrade the kitchen counters and appliances. I called her and told her that wouldn't fly. Sure the appliances weren't brand new but a little elbow grease and some oven cleaner would fix the stove right up. The fridge just needed to be cleaned as well. As I expected Mr. Thomas almost went through the roof when I emailed him the offer. Due to Mr. Thomas's hectic work schedule I had to take his calls at any time. I can remember trying to talk to him just as I turned into Taco Bell with three hungry kids in the car. Then to complicate things further Mrs. Thomas, who didn't speak English very well, kept asking him what I was saying. I'm sure the background noises on my end contributed to her confusion. It seemed to take an hour but I got his counter offer and managed to keep my sanity.

We got the offer worked out and scheduled the closing. Mr. Thomas traveled frequently and in spite of my best efforts he found out he would have to leave the country the day before closing. I almost collapsed when he broke the news. I called the attorney's office to see what could be done. They suggested a power of attorney which we were going to do for Mrs. Thomas anyway. The paralegal emailed the documents to the Thomas' but forgot to check on it after that. Mr. Thomas was out of town yet again and his wife had trouble understanding the instructions in the email. We got down to two days before and she still hadn't sent anything back. Mr. Thomas was upset with the staff at the attorney's office but I explained what would happen if we didn't get their paperwork back. He was able to calm down and orchestrate everything so we could close on time.

7 YOU WIN SOME...

Every agent has a listing that for some reason, besides every marketing trick in the book just will not sell. I had several over the years so I'm no exception. The first time it happened I was confused and frustrated. As time went on I learned not to be bothered by it because we can't predict the future. When a friend of mine was looking for her house we saw one on the outskirts of the county twice. I was the only agent that showed it twice so the owner called me and asked if I would list his house. I was still green so I agreed before I did my research. The owner, Jim, insisted his listing with his current agent was up and I had nothing to worry about. A few days went by and MLS still said it was 'active' so I called the other agent. She seemed surprised that her client was trying to replace her. She told me, "Well, I would rather you have it before anyone else." I think that was a compliment. She released him from his listing immediately.

The house sat on several acres so when I went out to take pictures I dressed accordingly. Not to mention they had two humongous dogs that followed me everywhere. The previous agent's pictures looked as if they had been taken from the road leading up to the house. The interior didn't have very many shots either but the virtual tour filled in some of the blanks. I was talking to Jim's wife Sara about their previous experience. She said they had asked for the pictures to be retaken but the other agent never came back. Out of curiosity I asked how the other agent had been dressed when she came out and took the pictures. Sara confirmed my suspicion, "She had on heels and a dress." I smiled and said, "She took so many photos from the driveway because standing in the grass would mess up her shoes. Plus the dogs would have had a field day with that dress." We laughed but it was true. Property like Jim and Sara's needed lots of pictures from different angles to show all the features of the land.

The house was outside the city limits but it wasn't that far from shopping centers and several nice restaurants. I wrote the description for MLS after many painstaking revisions. We didn't get many showings at first but I reassured Jim and Sara that we were going into the slow holiday season. Spring was just around the corner and Sara was getting more anxious by the day. She and I had a long talk one afternoon and I stressed the importance of reducing the price but she didn't want to "give" her house away. Two days later she called me to say she wanted to list with someone else. I was shocked because I thought we had come to an understanding a few days before. She kept saying it wasn't anything personal but she had a friend that was in real estate and she thought it was time for a fresh set of eyes. I didn't argue and I told her I would leave a form to terminate the listing at the front desk in my office. She could stop by on her way home from work and sign it. I went out that afternoon and got my lockbox and signs.

Six months went by and Jim called me again. It seems he hadn't been on board with Sara's decision but she talked him into it. He said the listing expired and the one and only time

Sara's friend had come to the house or called was when she
listed it. After that they didn't hear another word. I agreed to
list the house again and this time I took a fresh approach.
Since we couldn't get the agents to show the house I decided
to bring them in with something they couldn't refuse; free
food. We set a date for the Realtor luncheon and I told Jim
and Sara several times what to expect. The day before I was
running all over the place and I forgot to call them and
remind them. I called the morning of the luncheon on my
way to the office and left a message. Jim called back and I
could tell he had been asleep. It was 9:00 in the morning and
that wasn't a good sign. He said Sara had to leave town
suddenly to visit a sick relative and he had forgotten all about
the luncheon. He said he would vacuum and straighten up as
best he could but he still hadn't finished some of the items on
the list I gave him.

My broker told me I should cancel it but it was too late. I
had one hundred pieces of fried chicken, two pans of green
beans, two pans of macaroni and cheese, dozens of rolls and
gallons of sweet tea in my back seat. What was I going to do
with all of that food?! I had come too far to turn around. I
put out signs so people wouldn't get lost and I soldiered on.
Surprisingly we had a great turn out. I thought the distance
would be a problem. Several agents from my office came and
a few of them helped me set up. I was grateful because I felt
increasingly overwhelmed with each trip to the car to bring
stuff into the house. Some of the agents made negative
comments but some saw the possibilities and potential. Some
of them mentioned the upgrades looked as if they had been
done as weekend projects and they lacked a professional
finish. Those were objections I couldn't deny or overcome.

I tended the food, served desserts and schmoozed with my
fellow Realtors until the last person left. Then I put all the
leftovers back in the containers, put plates for Jim and his
kids in the fridge and loaded my car. I figured with Sara out

of town making sure they ate a good dinner was the least I could do. I had peace that I had done all I could, literally and figuratively, to sell their house. A few months later we got an inquiry from someone in my office. She had taken a woman out to look at the house and it was love at first sight. We thought we had a fighting chance until the husband found out the entrance was a private road with shared maintenance responsibility among the neighbors. He flatly refused to even drive out and look at it. None of us could recover from that one. When the listing expired Jim and Sara said they were going to take a break for a while and I agreed it was probably for the best.

My next mission impossible was an executive style home in an older area of town. I knew this lady through a friend and working with her and her husband taught me some valuable lessons. Claire and Michael were upper class professionals. Michael owned a business and Claire worked in the legal field. They never told me why they wanted to sell their house and many details weren't clear until months later. Originally I thought she and Michael were downsizing because their children were grown. The truth was Michael and Claire did need to downsize but not for the reasons I thought.

The house had been in rough shape when Michael and Claire bought it and the seller had made some patch repairs. When I checked the MLS history the house had been listed many, many times but only sold twice. There was evidence of water damage and several minor things that had turned into big projects. From the beginning I had trouble getting Claire to set a price that would get the house sold quickly. When people are emotionally attached to something they see value in a distorted way. What they're actually trying to put a price on are their memories and that is impossible to do. Appraisers couldn't care less if you have Great Aunt Martha's antique crystal chandelier in the dining room or Italian marble tile in the foyer. They compare square footage, age and construction style just to name a few when they appraise value.

Another hurdle to overcome was the mixed age of the homes in the surrounding neighborhoods. The houses were built anywhere between 1975 and 2005. It was a nightmare to get Claire to see that older houses had to be the best horse in the race to get attention. I held the first open house the same weekend as a city-wide open house campaign. The traffic was incredible, the weather was beautiful and the balloons I put out pulled in the crowds. Claire was elated when I told her how many people had come through. I followed up with all the guests but none of them were interested and some didn't even remember coming. That was not a good sign. We had some more showings but none of the feedback was favorable.

We went into the holidays and I did another open house at the first of the year. Since I was working in new construction at the time I never considered people might not come out when it was cold. And that day turned out to be the coldest day of winter yet. I thought about canceling but I had already put an ad in the local paper. By now Claire had told me what was really going on and I totally understood. She didn't want to give up her dream house but it didn't look like there were any other options. It was the beginning of hard times for many business owners and Michael hadn't been exempt. While I was waiting on people to come by I prayed for Michael and Claire while I walked through their house. I went from room to room and I stumbled onto a photo album full of family pictures. Then it hit me and I knew what the problem was. Claire was fighting me so hard because she hadn't detached from the house yet. Every closet was still full and nothing had been packed up. As long as she was holding on there wasn't much I could do to help her.

Claire complained to our friend that I wasn't giving her house the attention it deserved. She failed to realize that I had invested many dollars into marketing that my company wasn't paying for. I was in new construction when she met me and there were certain things I was required to do for the neighborhood I was assigned to. It wasn't that my attention was divided; I just couldn't convince anyone to buy her house. They took one look at the water damage, the rotten wood and the high maintenance exterior and went running in the other direction no matter what I said. Then I heard her house had been stigmatized. The term 'stigmatized' means a major event with a negative connotation has made a property famous or infamous as the case was with Claire's house. Many people remembered all the water damage from before Michael and Claire bought the house. Some of them didn't think I was being honest when I said the roof had been replaced. I was fighting a losing battle. After a year and only two price reductions the listing expired and the house was acquired by an investor that made all of the repairs and rented it out.

That experience taught me that some people don't care that you have to take on other clients and responsibilities to make a living in this business. If they stand in the way of you helping them to accomplish their goal they will still blame you. As I said before, selling a home is an emotional process. It can get even more complicated when you're emotionally attached and you have to sell because of some sort of distress. If your Realtor knows your situation they can be more effective. At the same time you have to trust their expertise and take their suggestions. We see dozens of houses every day in various conditions. We sometimes know when a house won't pass an appraisal or a home inspection. It's our job to prepare to overcome as many of the potential objections as possible. If you think you know more than your Realtor then you may end up losing money while your home sits and you get deeper into a hole.

My next clients wanted to sell and be closer to the husband's job. Lionel and Vickie owned a very unique house in a historic section of town. It was situated on a hilly lot that made part of the yard unusable. It had a walk-out basement but it was built into the side of a hill. It was a very unusual house for this part of the country. The view from the living room was amazing but the floor plan was oddly laid out. There wasn't a true hallway in the house and all the bedrooms opened into the family room or the back of the breakfast area. The laundry room was in the basement and that was a turnoff for many buyers. Lionel wasn't realistic about his price but there were extenuating circumstances that prevented us from pricing the house accurately. The best feature was a large screened porch that ran the length of one whole side of the house.

Showings were complicated because Lionel and Vickie didn't want to leave the alarm system off. They didn't want the code given out and they chose not to get an alternate code just for agents to use. This meant one of us had to go over and turn it off before showings then go back and turn it on again afterwards. Many agents hate alarms and when a house has one some of us may skip it rather than deal with the hassle. As long as sellers told me where the panel was I didn't mind disarming them. Lionel was willing to offer all kinds of incentives to get activity up but he flat out refused an open house. Without being able to lower the price and the complicated showing instructions the house expired before I could sell it.

The week before it expired I tried to extend the listing but Lionel gave me the run around. On the day the listing expired he called my office and demanded the sign and lockbox be removed before the close of business. When I got the message from the office I was stunned. I went over and got my signs but I had no way to leave the key and lock the house up because of the type of lock on the front door. I took the lockbox and decided to go back before church that night and return the keys when someone was home. I rang the doorbell and Lionel looked shocked to see me when he answered the door. I told him the truth, "I wanted to make sure you got your keys. Have a good evening." I turned around and walked away as Lionel slowly closed the door. He listed with a franchise that promised to buy your home if they couldn't sell it. Six months after that it was listed with someone else. To my knowledge he changed companies two more times and even attempted to sell it himself over the next year and a half.

8 NEW BEGINNINGS

I'm sure you're curious to know what happened with our house. Things got rough in 2010 and we struggled to pay all our bills. I called the company that financed our truck and asked what our options were to avoid repossession. They explained we could restructure our payments for six months and that would be the best option given my unpredictable income. So we signed an agreement and our payments were temporarily reduced by $200 per month. That gave us a little breathing room but we still struggled to pay our mortgage. After our tax refund was gone we got behind again in March. We got all kinds of letters from the mortgage company and one of them was an application for a loan modification. The government had several programs to help with modifications so I was praying we would qualify for one of them. I sent the application back along with the documents they had requested.

I foolishly thought that was all I would be asked to do. Soon I had to send copies of the same documents over and over; profit and loss statements, bank statements, detailed lists of every bill we had to pay. I was distraught and all I could think of was imminent foreclosure. We waited for an answer but I continued to call and ask if there was something else we could do. Each time I called I was told our application was still being reviewed. I called my mentor almost every day and she did everything she could to encourage me. She even filled my truck up with gas one day out of the blue. God was still faithfully taking care of my needs. However I got very distracted by all the threats the enemy was sending. I cried and wept over my situation many days. I wish I could say I praised my way through.

In the meantime the calls and threatening letters from the collection division of the bank never stopped. They called us at least three times a week demanding to know when we could make a payment to bring our account current. I stopped talking to them because the more I tried to explain the more belligerent they became. My mentor told me to write them a letter back every time they sent me one. So I did and basically I just retold the same story but it was the truth. This went on for two more months until I called one day in June and was told our application for a modification had been denied. They didn't give an explanation and claimed there were no notes in the file giving a reason.

The phone calls and letters intensified after we were denied. By now, I had nothing else to try so I spoke to the customer service reps every now and then when they called. I had some civil conversations and one young man told me to call and tell them when I could make a payment. He said I could tell them I would have the payment in by the 30th to stop the automated calls and the more harassing ones that came after those. I thanked him and took his advice since we were only two months behind at that time. They kept offering us ridiculous "options" to get caught up. Usually it involved paying one and a half times our regular payment for six months to clear up the fees and penalties. My question was, if we can't pay the regular payment how are we going to pay a larger amount? It made no sense to me at all.

We coasted along for a couple more months until one day I got a call from a young lady with the nastiest attitude I had ever encountered. She badgered me relentlessly and I kept telling her we were doing all we could but the bank she worked for had denied our modification. She said, "Let me check the system. This is showing you have a surplus of $1,700 every month." I said, "What!? How is that possible?" She snapped back, "Ma'am this information came from the financial documents you provided." She caught me on the wrong day and I just went off. "Listen! I'm not arguing with you! I know what your computer says but I'm telling you what my pocket is saying. We don't have an extra $1,700 a month. If we did you and I wouldn't be having this conversation!!" She kept on undeterred, "When are you going to make a payment ma'am?" I said calmly, "I don't know." She said, "Well, you're already behind and the next step is foreclosure. You need to take care of this immediately…" I just hung up the phone while she was still talking. I decided to go back to our bankruptcy attorney for another free consultation. I wanted to make sure I wasn't missing anything.

When I went to the appointment it was a very humbling experience. I filled out a budget worksheet listing all of our bills and debt. When Mr. Garner came in we caught up for a few minutes and in six years he hadn't changed at all. He was still a man of integrity and great Christian character. He looked over my worksheet and scratched his head. He looked me in the eye and said, "Well, you haven't been living extravagantly. You've been very modest in your spending and purchases." I told him we had purposefully stayed out of the credit card trap. After bankruptcy we had worked hard to get our credit back in shape. Mr. Garner looked over the paperwork again and said, "Well, what's putting the most pressure on you?" I explained about the house and how we had been denied a loan modification. We didn't have anything else that was financed except our car. I had two department store cards and a MasterCard but all the balances together were less than $4,000.

Mr. Garner sat back in his chair and shook his head, "I've seen a lot of people get into trouble with these loan modifications. Mostly because the bank draws the process out and some banks even tell the people not to make payments while they wait on a decision. Then before they know it they're in foreclosure. It's a sticky situation once you get in it." I agreed, "That's what happened to us. We kept making payments when we could while we waited to hear back from them though. We just couldn't make them on time every time." Mr. Garner nodded and said, "Well, the law says you can't file chapter seven again but you could do a chapter 13. Based on the bills you have here I have one concern and that's your vehicle. For the age of it and what you still owe I would look at trying to trade it in to get something a little newer." I could see Mr. Garner's point but anything that would seat the five of us comfortably and safely wouldn't be any less expensive.

Mr. Garner sighed and read over the worksheet again. He did some quick calculations and wrote out an estimate of what our monthly payments would be on a chapter thirteen plan. He looked up at me and said, "Well, you know how this goes. I'm going to send this packet home with you, talk to your husband and see what he says." I thanked Mr.

Garner for his time and I called Steve on the way home. Between the legal fees and charges we would have to pay just to file bankruptcy again it was not a practical option. We had borrowed money to file the first time and this time it just didn't make sense. The mortgage was the only thing we were having difficulty with. I continued praying to God and waiting for Him to show me what to do.

A little while after that I went to a midweek bible study at the church that has since become our church home. Instead of studying the regular lesson we were told we would pray corporately instead. The associate pastor told us to write down anything we wanted to ask God for and we would lay it on the altar. I took out a piece of paper and thought for a few minutes before I started writing. I thought about all the needs we had. Obviously the house and provision for the kids' school clothes and supplies were at the top of my mind. I walked up to the altar and dropped my prayer list in the huge stack with everyone else's. When I got back to my seat I prayed and cried out to God until I started to weep. Finally, the benediction was prayed over us and I left feeling peaceful.

A few weeks later I had already forgotten about my prayer and waiting on God. My emotions wanted to find the easiest way to get out of the anguish I was experiencing. I wanted to try and sell the house but Steve refused. With property values where they were we wouldn't be able to make enough off the sale to cover the mortgage balance. I asked about doing a short sale or a deed in lieu of foreclosure but the house had to be actively listed on the market for six months before the bank would even consider it. The closings I had in July got us caught up on our other bills but I could only make one mortgage payment. By then we were so far behind it was about to be counted as the third month and the bank wanted all the late fees, penalties and payments brought current. I went to my new broker one day and asked him to help me. He made a few calls to his friends in the mortgage industry and he called me into his office a few days later. "Here's what you need to do," he said. "Call the mortgage company and ask for the loss mitigation department. You've been talking to collections and you won't get anywhere with them. You'll have to be persistent and they may try to give you the run around. Tell them you only want to talk to loss mitigation."

The first time I called and asked to be transferred to loss mitigation I was told they couldn't transfer me due to the high call volume that department received. They said I would have to wait for someone to call me back. I hung up and called right back to try again with someone else. When I did get through it was a recording that said I would have to leave a message. I tried many times and talked to some people that said they were in loss mitigation but sounded a lot like the collections people. They said we couldn't apply for a modification again since we had already been denied. One day in August I got a call from a lady named Ms. Simpson in the bank's loss mitigation department. She said she needed more information from me and her boss, Mr. McDonald, was looking over our file to see what could be done. I gave her the information she requested and waited for her boss to call me back.

When Mr. McDonald called back he asked if any of our monthly bills had increased since we originally submitted our modification application. Several of them had so I gave him updated amounts. He said he would run the numbers and call me back. He was optimistic that he might be able to help us. We hung up and I walked around the house praying and thanking God. Mr. McDonald called me back with a few more questions. Then he asked me to hold on while he made some quick calculations. When he came back to the line he said, "I think we can help you. We can reduce your interest rate to 2% for five years and it will gradually build up to 4.375%." Then he gave me the new payment amount and asked, "Do you think you can handle that?" I said, "What about the taxes and PMI insurance?" Mr. McDonald said those amounts would stay the same. I told him we could probably make the new payments. He said he would get his boss to sign off on it and send us the paperwork by an overnight carrier.

I called everybody that we trusted with our situation and told them the news. Steve was overjoyed but I was still concerned about the final payment amount. About two weeks later we still didn't have anything from the bank so I called Mr. McDonald again. He assured me that everything was okay and the department sending us the paperwork was probably backed up with requests. Sure enough the overnight envelope was on my front porch a few days later. The final payment amount was about $800 less than the original and I was relieved. The private mortgage insurance was the biggest chunk of it but it couldn't be lowered. With the principal, interest, taxes, PMI and homeowner's insurance it would still be a lot of money every month. We got the paperwork notarized and sent it back in the self-addressed envelope they provided. I dropped it in a pickup box and prayed this was the end of the whole thing.

When October came we made our first new payment with no problem. Our modification on our auto loan was up so we were back to the full payment on it every month. By the time we had to make November's payment it wasn't so easy. It wasn't long before we were behind again. When I thought back over the past year I knew I had to put my trust in God and believe He would make it work out for our good. In the midst of everything else that was going on we were going through a spiritual transition. We found ourselves looking for a new church home for the first time in almost six years. Everything we were experiencing was scary and unfamiliar but we knew we had to walk through it together.

We made some mistakes and a few times we failed the test of giving God his tithe over paying our bills. We didn't always agree about which option was the right thing to do. Each time we had to make a choice the aftermath let us know whether we chose correctly or not. I had to believe that even though it felt like we were having déjà vu it was my perception that needed to be adjusted. We went on our first corporate fast together with our new church. I saw God do some amazing things in twenty one days. Towards the end of that time I went to a women's bible study meeting that was part of my mentor's ministry. While she was telling a story I've heard her tell half a dozen times before I got a whole new revelation.

There was a time when she wanted to buy her sister's car. She prayed about it and God gave her a figure that she would pay. When her sister decided to sell the car my mentor asked what price she wanted and what her sister said didn't match with the amount God said. So she went home and thought that was the end of it. Her sister put an ad in the paper and never said anything else about the car. A few months later my mentor went to visit her sister and was bracing herself because she just knew the car had been sold. Imagine her surprise when the garage door rolled up and the car was still inside! So she tried to play it cool as she asked her sister, "What happened? I thought you put an ad in the paper." Her sister explained that a buyer had never come along so she just kept the car. My mentor could barely contain her excitement.

She asked again about buying the car and her sister said, "You know I thought about it and maybe the price I was asking was a little high. I tell you what, I'll sell it to you for $____." My mentor almost lost it because the figure was exactly what God said to the penny. One day her daughter wanted to run a quick errand so she let her drive the car. A little while later she got a phone call from her daughter saying she had been in an accident. The car was totaled. She grieved over the car for a while and asked God why her car had to be destroyed. He gave her a surprising answer when He spoke this to her. "I said it was your car and I even told you how much you would pay for it. I never said how long you would keep it."

Once again we found ourselves facing a delinquency with our mortgage. I called and asked about a short sale and they mailed a packet for us to fill out. I read over the paperwork and realized we couldn't submit it until we actually had a qualified buyer. We were expecting our tax return so we decided to just prepare the house for the market and get caught up when our money came. Unfortunately the day the money should have been in our account came and went. I went online and the IRS web site gave me a different date. Then that date came and went. I was beyond frustrated.

I had originally told our mortgage company that we would be caught up on the 25th of February but because we didn't get our money that didn't happen. After I realized it would be another week before we could make a payment I called them back to explain why I had not kept my word. The customer service rep was friendly and after I told him what happened he transferred me. A young lady came on the line and said she needed to ask me a few questions. She wanted to get updated information on our expenses. I was confused because I couldn't see what all of this had to do with us being late on our payments. I gave her the information she requested and then she said we were $900 in the hole from her calculations. She said our best option would be to apply for another modification. I was speechless. She explained that within ten days a package would be sent out for us to complete. In the end, that young lady was wrong. The rules are very different when you've already had one modification.

Even though I usually had no idea where the money was coming from or when it would show up I called our lender every month. I told them I intended to pay them and I gave them a date for when I hoped to be able to fulfill my obligation. I had done everything I could to prepare in the event we would have to leave our home. I looked for homes we could rent; cleaned our house like the president was coming and tried to make some minor repairs as frugally as possible. In the end, it was like Abraham's experience when he was about to sacrifice Isaac. God wanted to see if my heart was ready to follow Him no matter what.

EPILOGUE

By the spring of 2011 I had gotten a part time job at a local hospital. I worked in a department that had to be manned around the clock so my hours varied every week. They were still short-staffed even after I was hired so my first few paychecks were great from covering open shifts. Soon two more people got hired and by the summer I was only averaging 32 hours or less every two weeks. I had grown tired of working every single Saturday and Sunday night and still not having enough money to get out of the hole. Steve suggested I tell my boss I was available during the week so I could get more hours but the people with seniority were chosen first. With no money to spare I had to let my real estate license go inactive because I couldn't pay the $475 fee to keep my MLS membership. It was heartbreaking but I didn't have a choice. Some of the clients I was working with hadn't been able to secure financing due to the newly tightened lending regulations. Some others had grown frustrated by the bounty of decent foreclosures that couldn't be financed by FHA and decided to hold off on buying.

Right after the kids went back to school I was contacted by my former employer. They wanted to know if I would be willing to come back to work. This was something I had to think long and hard about. When I left I had absolutely no intentions of ever going back. I prayed and consulted godly counsel before I finally agreed to do it. I told my supervisor at the hospital that I would stay on until the first of the year. I went back to work full time the day after Labor Day in 2011. I never in my life imagined I would have two jobs but there I was doing it.

One night we got a call from someone that identified herself as a bank employee. She asked me some questions about our loan modification. I told her we had asked about another modification but the bank's rules were strict. We would have to wait a full year and be caught up on our payments to even be considered for another modification. Since we were two months behind they wouldn't agree to it. The lady said her name was Lorie and she was very kind. She gently suggested we put the house on the market because it was time to face the inevitable. I told her that my husband and I weren't really in agreement on it so she said she would check on some other options and call me back in a week. In the meantime, I had received a short sale packet from the bank months earlier when I was thinking about selling the first time so I decided to look for it. I read over the requirements for a short sale and deed in lieu of foreclosure to get a better understanding of the process. The bank wouldn't make it easy to do either one but the only other alternative was walking away. I thought we should at least give it a try. When I tried to call Lorie back a few days later they said they didn't have anyone in the collections or loss mitigation department by that name. I didn't know what to say but the scripture about entertaining angels came to mind.

We started packing up the house the next week. We cleaned the whole house from top to bottom and made some of the small repairs that we could afford. We really needed to paint the interior but some of the 20 foot walls made that impossible. We didn't have the money for that much paint or a professional painter. We tried to make the cleanliness overshadow the imperfections. I called my former brokerage the next day and asked for the agent on duty. Thankfully it was someone that always got awards for production every month. I told him I had already done the paperwork so all he had to do was come by to pick it up and put a sign in the front yard. By October 2011 we had the house on the market and we were optimistic. We had a couple showings the first three weeks but it was disappointing when the agents said their clients hadn't expressed any interest.

By December my mother was very upset over the conditions in her apartment building. She wanted to leave so desperately that she moved in with us. With no full bathroom for her on the main floor we knew we couldn't stay in the house much longer. My mother has health problems and she is on oxygen so having to climb stairs just to shower every night was not the ideal situation. I searched for a rental house in our area that would allow our kids to stay in the same school. I looked online and even applied for a house that was being managed by a broker I knew. Unfortunately because of our history of bankruptcy and the negative reports on our credit she wanted me to ask a relative to cosign the lease with us. She seemed to be in a hurry to get us to commit but she hadn't even let me see the inside of the house. Before I could make a decision she said two more couples had applied and their credit was better than ours. I thought that was the end of it but suddenly she started calling me again a week later. She was pressuring me to bring her a deposit so I told her we were going to keep looking.

I looked at a few more houses but there was a shortage of available properties that would meet our basic needs. I looked at a few apartments online but all of them required a credit check. Besides that Steve was against moving into an apartment anyway. Being a huge military community many of the rentals had been snapped up before I started looking.

Then one day I was checking a site I had visited before and I saw a new listing. The listing didn't give the address but from the map I knew exactly where it was. There were only three pictures but it looked like a good match for us. I rode by one morning on the way to work. There was no sign in the yard but all the blinds were pulled up and I could tell it had been very well maintained. I emailed the owner and asked what we needed to do to apply. He replied and said that I should give him a call.

When I spoke to Mr. Johnson I explained our situation and he didn't seem opposed to renting us the house. He did admit they weren't prepared for the overwhelming response his online ad generated. He promised to get back to me with an application as soon as the Realtor that was helping him supplied it. I was dumbfounded when the paperwork he sent looked identical to what I had filled out for the other broker a few weeks prior. I didn't worry about it because at least she could vouch for us and let him know we weren't a risk. A week later we found out the house was ours and Mr. Johnson even held it for us until we could get our deposit and first month's rent together. Favor was on our side. The house was exactly 2,000 square feet with a two car garage, fully fenced back yard and a little storage shed that was wired. The interior of the house had been painted; Mr. Johnson was providing a year's worth of air filters for the HVAC and paying to have the yard sprayed for weeds every month. We moved in the week after Christmas.

A few weeks after we moved I was ready to put my stress to an end so I called and asked about the deed in lieu of foreclosure since we had been on the market for the length of time the bank required. Much to my surprise we got an offer on the house the next day! The offer was ridiculously low. We had already priced the house $40,000 below market value but it really didn't matter. The bank was making all the decisions anyway. We sent off all the paperwork and even more paperwork that they called and asked for. The buyers' agent wisely set a closing date for late March and I hoped we would have an answer by then. Short sales usually fall apart in the waiting process. The banks sometimes respond so slowly that buyers lose interest and move on. Weeks and weeks went by and the buyers' agent emailed my agent to say they were withdrawing their offer. I called the bank to see if this would get them to act but my call on Monday morning was never returned. When our case manager finally called my agent on Thursday the deal was long past dead.

A week later we got a letter stating the foreclosure sale of our house was set for May 1, 2012. I emailed my agent to let him know and to thank him for all of his hard work. I told him I didn't have any fight left in me where the bank was concerned. With May right around the corner I can't help but think the bank moved so slowly on purpose. They had someone contact our agent to get inside the house so they could change the locks weeks before the letter came. This person was also assigned to cut the grass. That doesn't sound like they were planning to do anything but foreclose. I wasn't angry or sad. We did all we could do according to the rules they gave us.

A few days later our agent called to tell us that he had another prospect for the house. I wanted to be excited but I couldn't muster it up. I told him we would cooperate with the bank and I would start gathering all the paperwork I knew they would ask for yet again. He told me to hang in there since we had about three weeks before the sale date. True to his word, our agent brought us an offer the following weekend. We quickly signed everything and returned it to him and the bank. Just like before it was hurry up and wait. The bank assigned our file to a processor that was very kind. She was helpful until she realized we had less than a week to the sale date. The processor tried to tell our agent that because of the type of Fannie Mae backed loan we had there was no way to get the deal worked out or stop the sale. Our agent was relentless and he convinced the processor to present our case to the committee of executives. Once again we received a miracle when they not only accepted the offer but completely stopped the foreclosure sale on April 27, 2012 exactly four days before it was supposed to be sold to the highest bidder. My God is awesome!

Thinking the worst was behind us we were beyond excited. Then we found out the bank was going to take anywhere from 10 to 30 days to complete the process. Slowly, there was progress. We were assigned to the same case manager as before, much to my dismay. With a tentative closing date set for the third week in May, all we could do was hope it was over before the end of the month. Again, we were at the mercy of the bank. They did finally get everything fully approved and the closing date was pushed back to the first week of June. The buyer had to get all the utilities back on to complete the home inspection and that was our last hurdle. We closed in mid-June and I didn't feel any sadness or remorse for how our dream house chapter ended. I know we'll be homeowners again someday and it will be even better than our dream house!

ABOUT THE AUTHOR

Kimberley W. Bush or Kim as her friend's call her, was born and raised in Montgomery, AL. She is married to her high school sweetheart, Steven. They have been married over 20 years and have three teenage children. Kim maintains a blog at www.kimbfearless.com and works alongside her husband in the family business. At the time of this writing, she has no plans to go back to real estate but hasn't completely ruled it out. She spends her spare time writing, feeding her passion for makeup with YouTube videos and interacting with people via her social media accounts.

www.ingramcontent.com/pod-product-compliance
Lightning Source LLC
Chambersburg PA
CBHW060403050426

42449CB00009B/1885